# AQUAPONICS

*Beginner's Guide To Building Your Own Aquaponics Garden System That Will Grow Organic Vegetables, Fruits, Herbs and Raising Fish With Your Own Aquaponics Home Gardening System*

By
Rachel Martin

© **Copyright 2019 by Rachel Martin - All rights reserved.**

The information provided within this book is offered with the intent of giving pertinent information concerning the topic of Aquaponics and all efforts have been attempted to make sure that the information is correct, makes sense, and will aid in accomplishing the intended purpose of this book. In any case, your acquisition of this book, in any format, specifically denotes your understanding that any information provided to you here to forth within the pages of this book are solely the expressed thoughts of the author and/or the publisher and is not meant to be construed as expertise in any given subject discussed. That being said, all information expressed on the subject matter within this book, is specifically done so with the intent of your enjoyment. There are many experts in the Aquaponics industry, some of which is discussed in the book and it is suggested that prior to moving forth with implementing any of the setups and or purchases discussed within the pages of this book, you take the time to review some of the advice those professionals offer.

According to the American Bar Association and the Committee of Publishers Association, everything detailed here is considered legal and binding throughout the United States.

It is illegal and punishable by the constraints of the law to copy, transfer, reproduce any part of the contents within this book. This is inclusive of duplicated renditions of this book in physical, digital and/ or audio versions barring direct authorization from the publisher to do so.

It is important to note that all information provided within this book is to be taken as words put forth with honesty and accuracy in terms of interpreting or portraying facts. Due to this fact, the publisher is free and clear of any liability when it comes to its use, whether used properly or not, especially when taken out of its direct intended purpose. To reiterate, there are absolutely no circumstances for which neither the author nor the publisher can be held responsible for outcomes resulting from the information provided within regardless of the gravity of said outcome.

Any and all information provided within this book has been provided with the sole intent of being informational material and held as universal consensus. Though informational and instructional in nature, any and all within this book is held as opinion, practice, and research of the author. Trademarks potentially discussed without consent in writing are not and cannot be construed as permission from the person in possession of said trademark.

# TABLE OF CONTENTS

Introduction .................................................................................... 1
Chapter 1 *What Is Aquaponics?* ............................................................ 3
Chapter 2 *Why Aquaponics?* ................................................................. 5
Chapter 3 *The Master Plan Basics* ........................................................ 13
Chapter 4 *How to Create A Proper Aquaponics Environment* ............... 48
Chapter 5 *Nutrient Cycle & Bacteria* .................................................... 67
Chapter 6 *How to Do It Yourself* .......................................................... 71
Conclusion ..................................................................................... 91
Description .................................................................................... 92

# INTRODUCTION

Congratulations on purchasing *Aquaponics: Beginner's Guide To Building Your Own Aquaponic Garden System That Will Grow Organic Vegetables, Fruits, Herbs and Raising Fish with Your Own Aquaponics Home Gardening System* and we appreciate you doing so.

The subsequent chapters will discuss in detail everything you need to know about Aquaponics so that you can determine if Aquaponics is right for you. This guide will help you to get on the path to healthier, cost-effective living by giving you the knowledge and basics needed to easily develop your Aquaponics garden.

With the creation of "Farm to Table" restaurants being a new craze, it is no wonder that farming has taken on a whole new meaning. Not only are more and more people concerned with the environment and/or healthier lifestyles, but people are becoming increasingly concerned with the economy, how they can improve their financial well-being, or simply save money. The use of Aquaponics gardens at home addresses all of these concerns. Everyone knows how expensive fruits, vegetables, and fish can be. The negative effects of fast food craze caused major detriments to health, but its popularity continues due to time constraints and cost benefits. Aquaponics helps us get back to healthy eating while saving time and money!

Through Aquaponic gardening, you can produce plants faster and larger without watering, weeding, and worrying about unhealthy chemical additives. In addition to plants, you have the option to eat fresh fish, right from your own tank.

Aquaponics has taken what Mother Nature has done for centuries to keep plants and animals coexisting and thriving and has allowed us to mimic that process at our own homes, whether indoors or out!

With numerous books available to purchase on this topic, we want to thank you for selecting this particular one. We have put forth a diligent effort to ensure that it is packed with a plethora of information that we believe will prove very useful to you, so it is our hope that you enjoy it!

# CHAPTER 1

## *What Is Aquaponics?*

Aquaponics is essentially a system in which fish and plants work together so that both can thrive. The two are cultivated together by way of a system built that utilizes recirculation of its natural biological processes. This ecological system involves waste production from the fish to be processed by bacteria and repurposed into necessary plant food that will then clean the water for the fish. Each plays a helping hand in the Aquaponics system that allows people to have an abundance of environmentally friendly, healthy, fresh food sources of both vegetation and fish. This system was born from the combination of the best parts of Hydroponics and Aquaculture, while removing the negatives associated with both, such as chemical additives for fertilization, the need for discarding water, and filtration.

## HISTORY AND CURRENT USES

Aquaponics may be on the rise in familiarity and use amongst both commercial farmers and home growers, but it is certainly not a new concept. We simply get the privilege of using the new and improved, and much easier versions of Aquaponics. As they say, history repeats itself, and those that are wise will learn from those before us. It will never cease to amaze me how centuries ago, before technology, before machinery, before mass communication and social networks, our ancestors were able to create such great inventions that allowed their people to not just survive but thrive, in many areas where the environment seemed to be a major impediment.

In some form or another, Aquaponics was used throughout the continent in places like China's rice paddy fields, in Africa, in Italy, throughout the islands, by Native Americans, and the Aztecs in Mexico, to name a few. The Aztecs migrated to an area that is known today as Mexico City. The land there did not have good soil for farming and the inner areas were all marshes. In order to adapt to this unproductive environment, they created numerous rafts on the lake out of substances found in the area, such as reeds and mud. On the rafts, they made gardens that utilized the nutrients from the aquatic species in the water to feed the plants.

Back in the day when people lived off the land, (in some places, they still do), it was vital to observe nature, take its natural processes, and use it in all aspects of life. Because of these observations, we have Aquaponics today! It is also important to note that in third world countries - just like the Aztecs so many centuries ago - faced obstacles in their environment such as bad soil, lack of water, and many people were starving. Many organizations are stepping in and introducing Aquaponics due to their fast-food growth without much water and soil-free gardening capabilities. In addition to a much-needed food source, it offers healthier, cleaner eating with much-needed vitamins and nutrients to aid in improving immune systems and fighting illness. The added bonus: Helping to prevent disease in one part of the world, stops the spread of disease to other parts of the world!

# CHAPTER 2

## *Why Aquaponics?*

The basic understanding of Organic is that the food was grown according to specific guidelines determined by the USDA that forbid the use of insecticides as well as requires strict adherence to the conservation of biodiversity and maintaining the welfare of animals. Essentially, this refers to the way Agriculture is raised and processed. The regulations differ greatly in every country. United States' crops labeled organic needs to be raised free of synthetic pesticides, bioengineered genes (GMO's), and petroleum-based and sewage-based fertilizers. For livestock raised for the purpose of meat, eggs, or dairy products to be labeled as organic, they must have access to the outdoors for the majority of the day, daily. They must also be fed organic feed and cannot be administered any antibiotics, growth hormones, or any by-products of animals.

Additionally, if you choose to get locally grown food versus shipped organic, you are aiding the local economy. More money goes to the local farmer instead of to the expense of marketing, packaging, and distribution. In the U.S. alone, food will likely travel approximately 1500 miles and in order to maintain freshness during the trip, the produce is picked before it is ripe and will ripen during travels or the food is processed with preservatives or other processes in an effort to keep it from going bad prior to sale. This means that food purchased from local farmers will be fresh and have much more flavor.

By choosing to grow your own food at home, you are getting the benefits you would from both organic and locally grown and having the added benefit of saving money.

In order to fully grasp how immensely beneficial Aquaponics is and why you should use it, it is important to also know about its roots, Hydroponics and Aquaculture. By comparing the three different systems, understanding their purpose, and noting their advantages and disadvantages, you will have a much better idea of which system is best for you. I believe, that like myself, you will gain a deeper appreciation for what Aquaponics can do for you as a new home garden and fish cultivator and through experiencing Aquaponics, you may expand further either into business endeavors or into larger home systems.

## HYDROPONICS

Hydroponics is a soil-free system of cultivating plants. In this system, the plants sit directly in the nutrient-rich water or are placed in soil free media such as gravel where the water can easily flow through. Once the nutrients have been used by the plants, it is necessary to add more nutrients or recycle the water.

## AQUACULTURE

Aquaculture means water life and is, therefore, is a system of cultivating fish. This system is basically tanks or aquariums where fish can be bred and grown and requires constant filtration in order to maintain clean water where fish could live and thrive.

## AQUAPONICS

Aquaponics is a system that combines Hydroponics and Aquaculture to cultivate both fish and plants together in one harmonious ecosystem. In Hydroponics, it is vital to recycle the water and add much-needed nutrients for the plants and in Aquaculture, it is vital to have water filtration for your aquatic species. By combining the two, Aquaponics removes the need to waste water, filtrate, and fertilize. Additionally, time and energy are reduced in the process.

It may just be the perfect marriage, but as in any marriage, there is some work involved in keeping everyone happy and healthy. In the end, it is all worth it. This union has created so many positives that make the negatives insignificant. In addition, it is outweighed by the benefits.

The following chart will show the benefits and drawbacks to all three:

## COMPARE AND CONTRAST

Based on the chart provided, it is clear that there are pros and cons to all three and it really is up to the individual as to which system they prefer, but in my opinion there is really no reason to look anywhere else but to Aquaponics for my cultivation needs.

For the purposes of this book, we will clarify what has been pointed out in this chart

| SYSTEMS | BENEFITS | DRAWBACKS |
|---|---|---|
| HYDROPONICS | NO SOIL NEEDED | CHEMICAL FERTILIZERS |
| | FAST GROWTH | TIME INTENSIVE |
| | MAKE BETTER USE OF SPACE AND LOCATION | DAILY MONITORING |
| | CLIMATE CONTROL REMOVING SEASONAL BARRIERS | SYSTEM FAILURE THREATS |
| | CONTROL OVER WHAT PLANTS EAT | EXPENSES |
| | CONTROL OVER pH | LONG RETURN PER INVESTMENT |
| | NO WEEDS OR PESTS | DISEASES AND PESTS MAY SPREAD QUICKLY |

### Hydroponics Pros and Cons

There is no soil needed in a hydroponics system. It produces fast growth of plants while making better use of space and location. Hydroponics is climate controlled so it, therefore, removes any seasonal barriers that one would experience in a regular garden or farm. You have complete control over what your plants eat because you have to feed them nutrient concoctions or chemical fertilizers daily. You have control over pH levels. There are no weeds because of the lack of soil and the use of insecticides removes the potential for pests.

On the flip side, chemical fertilizers may be great for your plant growth but they may not necessarily be safe for human ingestion and therefore a vigorous washing process must be undertaken. Hydroponics is time-intensive and requires daily monitoring. It is important to conduct system checks throughout the day because a system failure can be catastrophic to your production. Hydroponics is not easy on the wallet. It can get quite expensive to maintain and the return on your investment may take quite a long while to occur. As mentioned before, pesticides may be used but would defeat the purpose of healthy produce so other measures would need to be taken to ensure pest control. If pests or diseases do show up, the spread in this type of environment can be extremely fast.

| SYSTEMS | BENEFITS | DRAWBACKS |
|---|---|---|
| AQUACULTURE | SOURCE OF FOOD FOR PEOPLE AND MARINE SPECIES | WATER IS DISPOSED OF |
| | SOURCE OF INCOME | WASTE OF NATURAL RESOURCE |
| | FLEXIBILITY TO BUILD FISH FARMS, TANKS, AND CAGES ANYWHERE | WASTE OF INVALUABLE PLANT NUTRIENT SOURCE |
| | RECIRCULATING SYSTEMS HELP REDUCE, REUSE, AND RECYCLE WASTE | PROPAGATION OF INVASIVE SPECIES |
| | REDUCE STRAIN ON NATURAL POPULATIONS | THREATS TO COASTAL ECOSYSTEMS |

| | |
|---|---|
| | DUE TO WASTE DISPOSAL/ POLLUTION |
| | CONTAMINATES WATER AND THREATENS HEALTH |
| | AFFECTS WILD FISH POPULATION |

## Aquaculture Pros and Cons

Aquaculture can be used as a source of food for both people and marine species. It is a source of income for many who provide fresh fish to fish markets and restaurants locally. It gives great flexibility to build fish farms, tanks, and cages anywhere. Systems created around the idea of recirculation help reduce, reuse, and recycle waste. Aquaculture has greatly reduced the strain on natural populations as fewer people are fishing and more people are breeding and raising the fish.

A major problem has occurred with the waste of water because many still have not incorporated recirculation into their Aquaculture setups. In addition to water waste, lack of recirculation would then waste valuable natural resources found in the water that is made by fish waste and waste of invaluable plant nutrient

source. Of course, there is also the argument about the propagation of invasive species and the threat to coastal ecosystems due to waste disposal and pollution. CDC states that this contaminates the water and threatens health.

*An Aquaponics Garden using Deep Water Culture*

| SYSTEMS | BENEFITS | DRAWBACKS |
|---|---|---|
| AQUAPONICS | SOIL FREE | MUST GAIN KNOWLEDGE OF FISH, PLANTS, AND MICROBES |
| | ABUNDANT CHEMICAL FREE CROP | INITIAL EXPENSES CAN BE HIGH UNLESS YOU ARE WELL EQUIPPED TO DO IT YOURSELF |
| | ABUNDANT FRESH FISH | ELECTRICAL OUTPUT IS HIGH UNLESS USING SOLAR POWER OR ANOTHER FORM OF |
| | NO WASTE | NOT ALL CROPS CAN BE GROWN IN AQUAPONICS |

| | |
|---|---|
| DENSER PLANTATION/HIGHER PRODUCTION | SALTWATER FISH CANNOT BE BRED IN AQUAPONICS |
| STAGED PRODUCTION ALLOWS FOR YEAR ROUND HARVEST | MUST MONITOR NITRATE AND pH LEVELS REGULARLY |
| BACTERIA PRESENT MAKES THESE GARDENS IMMUNE TO DISEASE AND ARE SELF HEALING | |
| PRODUCE FISH AND PLANTS FROM SAME WATER SOURCE | |
| CAN BE CREATED ON ANY SCALE AND ANYWHERE | |

**Aquaponics Pros and Cons**

By combining the positive attributes of Hydroponics and Aquaculture and removing the negative aspects of the two, Aquaponics was born. It was not simply a merger but a major advancement into what could be possible not just for a few but globally! It is a soil and weed free environment that produces an abundant fresh fish harvest and an abundant lush rapidly growing crop. There is absolutely no waste because everything is re-circulated and utilized with never any need to discard the water. Instead of getting rid of water, you would occasionally add a bit of water due to evaporation. Denser plantation equates to higher production. Because you have the ability to stage your production, you can reap a bountiful harvest year round. The bacteria found in an Aquaponics system fight disease and help to heal in an effort to keep a healthy ecosystem. Fish and plants are produced from the same water source. Aquaponics systems can be created in a tiny little one or two fish tank with one plant to an enormous prosperous business farming fish and vegetation. Because of the fact that they can be created on any scale, and because of the simplicity in the requirements of the system, it can be located pretty much anywhere. Aquaponics gardens do not adversely affect the wildlife population. It will not be long before you are able to see a return on your investment.

To be successful in Aquaponics, it is very important to educate yourself about fish, plants, and microbes. Initial expenses can be high unless you are very well equipped and knowledgeable in doing it yourself. The electrical output is very high unless you are able to incorporate solar power or other forms of sustainable energy sources. Though the variety and list are long and getting longer every day with new advances, not all crops can be grown in an Aquaponics system. Additionally, though technically you can cultivate any fish, it is not recommended to do saltwater as that would require a lot more work and system additions as well as very selective plants (minimal options) in order to make that function effectively. Though the maintenance is not as laborious as the other two systems that make up the core of Aquaponics, there is maintenance involved that requires regular monitoring of pH and nitrates.

# CHAPTER 3

## *The Master Plan Basics*

It is important to determine what exactly you want to achieve with your Aquaponics system, how you want it to look, and where you want it to be located. Coming up with a plan is necessary to ensure that all pieces of the puzzle not only fit together but that there aren't any pieces missing. No one likes working on a puzzle for hours only to find that they can't finish what they started. This project has many stages: planning stage, supply stage, building stage, and testing stage, plant and fish stages (don't occur at the same time), maintenance stage, and for some, the expansion stage. I personally enjoy the sit back and enjoy or feast stage and yet others are more concerned with reaping the reward. Whatever the desired outcome, a plan is vital.

## DIY OR KIT

It is a matter of preference whether you choose to purchase a ready-made kit or do it yourself. Unless you happen to have a background in engineering or plumbing, I would strongly suggest that first time Aquaponics gardeners start with kits that are purchased from a very reputable company with knowledge and experience in Aquaponics. I stress this point because there are many kits on the market that can be bought pretty much anywhere and if you purchase it online from say a company like Walmart or Amazon, you would not have the ability to talk to anyone with expertise in Aquaponics that can help you choose the right system for you and answer any questions you might have. Further, after you have the system set up, it is good to be able to contact the company for any advice or assistance you may need. Your first kit is your opportunity to learn a great deal about Aquaponics as you are getting your feet wet. Purchasing a kit will remove much of the stress and allow you to enjoy what Aquaponics has to offer. If you choose to jump right in with a DO IT YOURSELF project, there will be a lot of trial and error, research, shopping around for supplies, and no direct contact person to aid you as you venture on this Aquaponics mission.

If you are able to find a kit that suits your needs and your wallet, go for it! It will allow you to get started on the road to a bountiful harvest much quicker, without the worry of troubleshooting the do it yourself project. DO IT YOURSELF can delay production by several months. The initial cost of purchasing a kit is worth it when you save time and money in the long run. DO IT YOURSELF can get expensive with the trial and error process one must endure plus you may not have all of the tools needed which is another purchase and of course the knowledge that is only gained over time to know exactly what supplies you need and which places are good to go (who you can trust) to get them from. Sometimes the simple task of purchasing supplies can be daunting because the Aquaponics supplies needed may not be easy to find. Kits come with everything you need to get started and are available for all sizes and levels of Aquaponics.

After you are used to Aquaponics and have a better understanding on how the system works and what it takes to be successful in Aquaponics, then you may choose to try your hand at a do it yourself project. Remember, Aquaponics is not for everyone and investing a lot of time and money in a do it yourself project initially doesn't make sense unless you are certain that Aquaponics is for you.

If you are an Aquaponics newbie and still choose to try your hand at a do it yourself project, you can buy excellent plans from reputable companies online and build it yourself. This would be the best option for DO IT YOURSELF Aquaponics first timers. If you have the time and skills, and choose the DO IT YOURSELF path, it can be significant savings for you. I pose the alternate point... If you attempt to DO IT YOURSELF and don't have the time and skills, you could end up spending considerably more as mentioned before.

Assuming that you chose to DO IT YOURSELF because you do have the time and skills, you have the distinct potential to customize the Aquaponics system to suit your needs and tastes. You will additionally benefit by gaining education about each part that you use to make your Aquaponics garden as you find out the intricacies of how they work and what they are needed for. Basically, DO IT YOURSELF leaves room for your inner creative soul to flourish and for those who enjoy the challenge of recycling and reusing, this could be very rewarding.

For the purpose of introducing readers to the basics of Aquaponics and how to create your very own Aquaponics garden, chapter 6 will delve into what DIY supplies are recommended and the best ways in which to connect the two worlds of fish and plants.

## INSIDE OR OUT?

A matter of preference really, as Aquaponics can be done basically anywhere. It is for you to decide what is best for you and the Aquaponics goals you would like to achieve.

For those that desire an inside garden:
- You have the freedom to maintain the temperature in accordance with the needs of your plants and fish
- You must have grow lights
- Size and appearance are dependent on location
- You need to make sure that the location you select can withstand the weight of your system when the tank/aquarium is filled with water

For those that desire an outside garden:
- No soil is needed but an excellent lighted area is important
- Must have close proximity to a water source
- Must have connectivity to an outlet for electrical source
- Will your system be in a greenhouse or will it need protection such as a fence or netting to ward off pests?
- Dependent on the climate where you live, a heating system may be needed to maintain proper temperatures

## SIZE AND APPEARANCE

For me, appearance is important, so the setup of my system is very important in that regard. I do not want it to resemble an industrial zone. This is my home, so I want to find a compromise between décor and function. Others may be more concerned with function and output and maybe with ease for productivity. Whatever your taste, putting the appearance aside, in Aquaponics, size does matter. It does not matter in barbaric terms of ah-hah mine is bigger than yours, but it does matter in regards to:

- What your ecosystem needs, in terms of ratios (example: plants to fish capacity)
- What your fish growth may be (remember, some fish like catfish get long and require much bigger tanks)
- Where your system is located (indoor area may not support large tanks)
- What you can afford overall (keep ongoing maintenance and utilities in mind)
- What your goals are (is this just a hobby? Is it just for ornamental purposes for both plants and fish? Or do you plan on expanding in the future?)

## PLANTS AND FISH LIVING TOGETHER

It is highly recommended to use freshwater fish since saltwater fish will restrict which plants you can grow in your garden.

In addition to determining whether you want to eventually eat your fish you simply want fish for ornamental purposes, you will need to determine what plants you want to grow because this ecosystem needs good matchmaking in order for the marriage to last. It is important to know:

- Does your fish require warm water or cool water?
- Can your fish survive in both temperatures? A few can acclimate to both.
- How big will your fish get?
- How many plant beds do you plan on having?
- Do you want cool weather plants or warm weather plants? Or do you want seasonal plants?
- What size fish will you get? (Fish fry, Fingerlings, or Adult fish)
- What are your local laws? There are restrictions on the types of plants and fish you can grow in each area.

Fish like Catfish, Bluegill, (Food fish) Koi and Goldfish (Ornamental fish) are pretty resilient and adapts easily to different temperatures making them the most popular fish for both the fish for food and fish for ornamental categories. Other fish like Trout and Tilapia which are also very popular Aquaponics breeds have very specific temperature needs. Tilapia require warm water (above 70 degrees) while Trout require cooler waters falling below that temperature.

Likewise, Leafy Greens, peas, cabbage, carrots, beets and spinach require cooler temperatures. Beans, squash, and sweet corn require warmer temperatures while tomatoes, peppers, eggplant, and melon are all seasonal (summer vegetation).

In order for your ecosystem to align harmoniously, choosing which plant or fish that goes well together is of vital importance.

## WHAT KINDS OF FISH-WORK IN AQUAPONICS?

The following fish have had the best results in Aquaponics systems:

- Tilapia
- Bluegill/ Brim
- Sunfish
- Crappie
- Koi
- Fancy Goldfish
- Pacu
- Ornamental Fish: Tetras, Angelfish, Mollies, Guppies, and Swordfish

These fishes are also popular Aquaponics fish that do well but may require more work:

- Carp
- Barramundi
- Silver Perch
- Yellow Perch
- Catfish
- Large Mouth Bass
- Cod (Murray, Sleepy)
- Salmon
- Rainbow Trout
- Minnows

It is important to note that nearly all freshwater fish are edible. The difference in each would be how easy it is to prepare, the taste, and health. Koi and Goldfish are not suggested as edible simply because they are known to carry cancer-causing factors that affect humans.

Another important determination is the size and age of the fish. Though the cost may be a big determining factor, it is important to note:
- Fish fry is cheaper, but it will take much longer to mature and thus will affect the nitrate production levels, taking longer to reach adequate supply needed for the plants to absorb.

- Fingerlings are expensive, but for good reason. They are ideal for waste production in early stages which results in expedited vegetable growth.
- Mature fish are the most expensive to purchase and cannot be mixed with fish fry as they will be eaten by the larger of the species. Additionally, larger fish require more plant beds and larger tanks.

Important to note: For a 100-gallon fish tank with a 100 gallon grow bed, the proper amount of fish would be about 12 to 15 pounds. The correct ratio would be one pound of fish for every square foot of grow bed volume, which amounts to approximately seven and a half gallons, if and only if you properly circulate the entire volume of water in the tank every hour on the hour.

When you harvest your own fish for the purpose of eating it as opposed to purchasing your fish from the store, aside from the convenience, of course, you have the added reassurance that your fish is fresh and safe. By raising the fish yourself, you have the distinct knowledge of what they eat and when it was harvested. You are the only one controlling every aspect of the environment, health, and growth of the fish which you consume. Additionally, the fact that they are cold blooded means that they are not susceptible to carrying harmful bacteria like E. Coli and Salmonella. The Center for Disease Control (CDC) is always monitoring and stressing that people need to be aware of potential risks of fish consumption because contaminants (such as mercury or polychlorinated biphenyls) from pollution (coming from industry, houses, or simply people) in the lakes, oceans, and rivers, work their way into the fish that reside there. This brings new meaning to "you are what you eat". By raising your own fish for consumption, you are removing any cause for concern because you know your fish are healthy.

Why is Fish consumption good for you? Fish that have white meat, more so than others, will have a lower fat content in comparison to other proteins sourced from animals. Fish that fall in the category of "oily fish", such as salmon, sardines, trout, mackerel, and bluefin tuna, are one of the best sources for good fats known as omega-3 fatty acids. Our bodies do not naturally create these vital nutrients in the quantities we need so it is very important to incorporate these into our diet through other sources and fish are not only a perfect source but a delicious one too!

- One of the healthiest foods out there
- Great source of abundant nutrients, protein, and vitamins (many people are highly deficient in vitamin D and this is a great source for improving that deficiency)
- Omega-3 fatty acids are essential for body and brain and scientifically proven to reduce the risk of numerous diseases. (They say an apple a day, keeps the doctor away, well a fatty fish or two a week, will give you all the omega-3 that your body requires).
- The fattier the fish, the better it is for us... super healthy!
- Whether you are pre-genetically disposed to heart attacks and/or strokes or you just want to do everything you can to avoid them (that would be all of us!), you can lower your risk of heart disease and other ailments simply by eating fish!
- Highly beneficial to children, fish contains DHA which helps development and growth.
- Researchers now state that eating fish regularly aids in the battle against deterioration in brain functions which tend to occur as people age. There is also evidence that grey matter of the brain is increased by consuming fish on a regular basis which would result in improved recollection and emotional status.

- Fish can not only make you healthier but studies have linked regular consumption to happiness and improvement in mental well-being.
- Source containing the highest level of vitamin D
- Fish is known to combat autoimmune diseases
- Studies show that when children consume fish regularly, it will help them combat asthma which will make it less likely to progress into adulthood
- Carrots are not the only thing recommended for eyesight. Fish has been studied in the battle against macular degeneration.
- Aside from the numerous health advantages linked to eating fish regularly, fish actually tastes amazing and comes in so many varieties. Fish is easy to prepare (for the most part) and there are so many recipes out there that you could literally not eat the same meal twice within the same year if you wanted the variety.
- Fish does not take long to cook and therefore those people who don't have a lot of time to spend on cooking their meals, fish is a great option.

**WHAT KINDS OF PLANTS WORK IN AQUAPONICS?**
The most common plants for Aquaponics gardens are:

- Leafy lettuce
- Bok Choy
- Kale
- Spinach
- Swiss Chard
- Arugula
- Herbs such as Basil, Coriander, Sage, Lemongrass, Parsley, and Mint

- Watercress
- Chives
- Common Houseplants

Other plants that do well but are dependent on a well-stocked fish tank are:

- Tomatoes
- Peppers
- Cucumbers
- Beans
- Peas
- Squash
- Broccoli
- Cauliflower
- Cabbage
- Eggplant
- Melon
- Fruiting plants such as Strawberries

Others have noted success with:

- Bananas
- Citrus trees like limes, lemons, and oranges
- Pomegranate

- Sweet Corn
- Microgreens
- Beets
- Radishes
- Carrots
- Onions
- Shallots
- Chili peppers
- Capsicum
- Celery
- Ginger
- Edible Flowers like Orchids and Violas

Why are vegetables good for you? Aside from being naturally lower in fat and calories and a major source of vitamins, minerals, and nutrients, there are many health benefits associated with the consumption of vegetables (and fruit too!)

- Vital for health and maintenance of the human body
- Reduces the risk of many chronic diseases
- An important source of potassium, fiber, folic acid, vitamin a, vitamin d
- Reduces blood pressure due to potassium
- Reduces cholesterol due to dietary fiber
- Reduces the risk of fetal defects in pregnant women due to the folic acid content
- Improves immune system
- Improves skin and eyes due to vitamin a
- Numerous benefits associated with vitamin c including oral health, iron absorption, and healing
- Reduces the risk of heart disease and illness associated with it
- Studies have shown that vegetables can combat specific cancers
- Healthy diets combat obesity and diabetes
- Combats Osteoporosis and some renal issues
- When eating more vegetables (and/or fruits) their high water levels aid in making you get the full feeling faster, and thus, help those that are trying to lose weight. It is low in

calories, in conjunction with this, helps us to stay well below the daily required caloric intake.

Whatever you choose to grow, always keep in mind the harmony of the ecosystem, the rate, and extent to which your fish or plants will grow. As mentioned earlier in this chapter, temperature and location are also very important factors in your selection process. It is vital to the success of the Aquaponics garden, that you take the time to learn about the fish and plants for your developing ecosystem.

**Some important things you should consider when selecting your plants and fish:**
Let's start with plants:

First, in considering which plants to purchase, especially if they are going to be used specifically for consumption, it is important to note that because you are utilizing water-based methods versus soil-based methods, your production rate at its bare minimum will be 20-25% higher. Therefore, due to the fact that you are yielding such high quantities, determine which vegetation you will use for farming and which vegetation you would be willing to incorporate preservation methods such as canning or dehydrating, like some like to do with herbs and fruit.

Second, the suitable range for most vegetables is 18 to 30 degrees Celsius which converts to a temperature range of 64.4 to 89.6 degrees Fahrenheit. Winter vegetables do best in temperature ranges of 8 to 20 degrees Celsius (46.4 to 68 degrees Fahrenheit). Summer vegetables will do best in temperature ranges between 17 to 30 degrees Celsius (62.6 to 86 degrees Fahrenheit). Within these ranges, different vegetables and plants have different requirements, though they may do fine within the range assigned to their seasonal type, the specific required range will yield the best results. Leafy greens, for example, fall in the winter vegetable category, however, they prefer even cooler temperatures than most, requiring temperature ranges between 14 to 20 degrees Celsius (57.2 to 68 degrees Fahrenheit), mostly after sundown. Following the winter vegetable guidelines of range, if they were exposed to increased temperatures near the higher portion of the range, the flavor of these vegetables would be negatively impacted and inedible to most. More important than air temperature is water temperature, which has a far greater effect on the plants, however, both are equally important to monitor.

Third, when growing flowering plants or plants that yield fruit, light is an important factor. Each requires different amounts of daylight and/or darkness to cause the flowering or fruiting process to occur. Medicinal plants and some peppers fall into the category of short-day plants. This means they need more darkness and others such as many ornamentals fall into the category of long day plants because they require much more light than others to yield their beautiful blooms. All plants generally come with care guidelines when you purchase them but it is important in your planning process to do this research ahead of time to ensure that you are prepared and have an action plan for your production goals. There are plants, like most vegetables, that are light neutral, which makes things a bit easier to maintain and control.

Fourth, I have listed quite a few plants used in Aquaponics but the list of plant growth success with herbs, small trees, vegetables, and flowers is up around 150 and growing. Knowing the needs of your plants and matching those needs to your fish properly will help you to expand your selection of plants and the success you have in Aquaponics. In saying this, always remember, the goal is to keep everyone healthy and fed—people, fish, and plants—so, to achieve this goal, we must understand nutrient requirements. Different species have different nutrient requirements—some need more, some need less. For example, if you are planning on growing fruiting vegetable plants like tomatoes, peppers, cucumbers, eggplants, avocados, or fruits like strawberries and winter melon, they require higher nutrient-rich diets so they are better matched with a well established Aquaponics system in which the fish are able to yield the amounts of nutrients they need. Additionally, amongst these various species are root crops. These plants are better suited for a system in which deep media beds are utilized and they are very high maintenance so it may not be a good choice for you to attempt in an Aquaponics system. Leafy greens, legumes, and herbs are the most popular choices for Aquaponics because they have a low nutrient requirement. In the center of the nutrient, demand spectrum would be things like cabbage, cauliflower or broccoli. Radish falls on the very low end of the spectrum while beets, onions, and carrots fall somewhere between the center of the spectrum and the higher side of the demand spectrum.

Fifth, some plants grow much larger than others. This is the case with fruiting plants. If space is an issue, keep this in mind when selecting your plants. Also, depending on the type of system set up you choose, this could influence greatly which plants you will be able to grow. For example, bulbous or root based plants are better suited for media based beds versus a nutrient film technique system or a deep water culture system due to the support system and growing environment needed for these plants to flourish.

Lastly, because of the variations in needs of the different plants, and likewise the varying needs of the fish needed to coexist with these plants for a balanced ecosystem, it is important to ensure balance in all areas to maintain balance overall! Mixing plants with different nutrient needs or harvesting timeframes, for example, could result in great imbalance for all of the creatures in the ecosystem as an attempt to compensate for differing needs. Any unbalance that cannot be easily corrected can cause the entire ecosystem to fail.

Notes: If you are planting something that requires a long term grow period, it would be a good idea to plant some short term grow period plants with them. This way you not only reap the benefit of farm to table on a regular basis but the plants work together. For example, eggplants take a long time to mature so adding in herbs, tomatoes, and leafy greens around them yields quickly for your main salad ingredients, and will offer shading to the eggplant that it needs while also working with the other plants to clean the water for the fish. This maintains a balanced nutrient level, thus creating a healthy environment. Smart planning in your planting design can not only be beneficial in maximizing space but it can also aid in attracting beneficial insects and greatly improve your plant production.

Obviously, there is a lot to consider when selecting your plants, whether you want them for food consumption or simply want a houseplant or flowering plant. Always keep in mind the harmony of all species in your ecosystem, when making your decisions. Obviously, the fish and the plants need to be a match made in heaven but the other important thing here, especially when it comes to foods we plan on consuming, is what you personally enjoy. I mean, let's be honest here, what is the point of all this work (except maybe satisfaction of achievement) if you aren't able to enjoy what you have produced? Why grow tomatoes if you don't plan on eating them? Why grow a flower you have allergies too? You wouldn't obviously. That being said, if you know that you eat certain vegetables very often such as the common salad ingredients or herbs that you need for seasoning your foods, you would be more inclined to select these options to grow and the amount that you grow would be higher than say an artichoke, which you may eat when you are in the mood for it. There is no rule of thumb here. Everyone has different tastes so I will not tell you what to put in the garden but simply offer knowledge about the different options and things to consider. To support this sentiment, I have put together some information that should prove useful in your Aquaponics vegetable planning below, but first I want to address the non-edible variety of plants. Edible varieties of plants are not the only plants well suited for Aquaponics, in fact, some of the best options for Aquaponics gardening are ornamental varieties of plants and Aquaponics is exceptionally successful in growing many kinds of houseplants. Roses are one of the most popular and successful of flowering plants, though there are many others that you can grow. House plants are a great way to keep the air clean and the house looking beautiful. Many varieties thrive in Aquaponics such as ferns and philodendrons, to name just two. You can pretty much grow just about anything from vegetables to plants to flowers, with proper environment set up, except blueberries and azaleas (due to their high acid needs) and of course the root crops like potatoes are really difficult to grow because of their need for a deep media bed, but even these, like carrots, for instance, have been grown successfully. The most effective and proven process for planting root based vegetables is that these should be planted in wicking beds which are attached to the media beds.

Ornamental plants have seen great success in Aquaponics gardens due to the constant flow of water and nutrients it receives. In addition to the roses, some great outdoor options are asters, lilies, daisies, forget-me-nots, hollies, and lavender.

Here is a list of some of the best options for indoor plants with information on whether you can use seeds or cuttings for best results:

- Spider Plants can be grown from either a seed or from cuttings.
- Female Dragon can be grown from either a seed or from cuttings.
- Chinese Money Plants can be grown from either a seed or from cuttings.
- Philodendrons can be grown from either a seed or from cuttings.
- Peace Lilies can be grown from seeds or from cuttings.
- Chinese evergreen can be grown from either a seed or from a cutting but it is suggested that you start with cutting because growing these from seeds is very difficult in Aquaponics systems.
- Devil's Ivy cannot be grown from seed but can be grown from cutting. Leopard Lilies, also known as Dumb Cane, cannot be grown from seeds but can be grown from cuttings. Arrowhead Vines cannot be grown from seeds but can be grown from cuttings.

The smell and taste of fresh herbs is absolutely amazing. My mouth is watering just thinking about it. Lucky for us, herbs are one of the easiest things to grow in an Aquaponics garden. Tarragon, Peppermint, Green Mint, Oregano, Basil, Sage, Stevia, Lemon Balm, Rosemary, and Cilantro are just some of the herbs you can grow and yes, you can grow from both seeds and cuttings, with the exception of Tarragon and Peppermint, but I strongly suggest always using cuttings because it gets your plants to grow stronger and faster. Lettuce, spinach, bok choy, tomatoes, peppers, cucumbers, and celery are some of the most popular Aquaponics choices and all can be grown from either seeds or cuttings, however, as I said earlier, I am going to go into further detail on vegetables and expand past this list so that you can have more information to help you make decisions when planning your garden selections:

Let's start with the leafy greens because they are the basis to almost any salad and there are so many varieties to choose from. This, of course, is why it is number one on the Aquaponics selection list. It grows fast and it is easy to maintain. Aside from this, instead of having to harvest the entire head of lettuce, leaving the unused portion in your refrigerator with the potential to wilt, you can simply go to your garden and pull the leaves off that you need at that moment. You not only get a freshly picked salad ingredient, but you allow the lettuce to continue to grow and remain healthy. So many perks to Aquaponics, trust me you will be hooked too. The leafy varieties are preferred over iceberg for two reasons other than taste preference. One, they pack more nutrients in them for our health and two, because they grow in only 30 days, whereas Iceberg takes 90 days. Remember what I said about making everyone happy in your ecosystem harmony? Well, we can't talk about our vegetables without at least giving a brief mention to our fish (I will get into them in greater detail later in this chapter). The majority of leafy green varieties prefer air temperature ranges between 60 and 80 degrees Fahrenheit. This is just the exposed part of our favorite lettuce. We cannot forget about the needs of the root system which is exposed to the water. As I said before, though both are important, the water is even more important and leafy greens prefer their water to be in the temperature range of 70 to 74 degrees Fahrenheit. (Here is where our fish friends get their brief mention) Tilapia happens to be one of the fish that is a perfect match for our lettuce to thrive because they too prefer their water to be in the temperature ranges of 70 to 74 degrees Fahrenheit. This covers all your leafy greens like spinach, watercress, and arugula as well as all your herbs such as chives, basil, and rosemary.

Let's break this down further:

- LETTUCE (MIXED SALAD LEAVES)
    - pH level ranges are 6.0 to 7.0
    - Plant spacing requirements are 18 to 30 cm (20 to 25 heads/m$^2$)
    - Germination time and temperature will be 3 to 7 days at 13to 21 degrees Celsius
    - Growth time is about 30 days (longer for some varieties like Iceberg)

- Temperature range is 15 to 22 degrees Celsius (flowering over 24 degrees Celsius)
- Light exposure needed is full sun
- Plant height is 20 to 30 cm tall and plant width is 25 to 35 cm wide
- Recommended Aquaponic method can be either media bed, NFT or DWC

The lettuce grows really well in an Aquaponics environment when nutrient concentrations in the water are more than sufficient. A number of them can be grown such as crisphead lettuce (iceberg), which has crispy leaves and a tight head, and is ideally suited for cool temps; butterhead lettuce has leaves that are loosely layered on another and tastes a bit sweet with no bitterness; Romaine lettuce has upright and tightly layered dark green leaves that are slow to seed and are sweet in taste; and loose leaf lettuce comes in a variety of colors and shapes with no head and can be directly planted on media beds and harvested by picking single leaves without collecting the whole plant. This allows for the plant to continue growth and for the grower to avoid having unused, harvested lettuce wilt. Lettuce is a winter vegetable, so it requires night temperatures to range between 3 and 12 degrees Celsius for head growth, and day temperatures to range between 17 and 28 degrees Celsius. Lettuce is highly dependent on light and temperature for proper growth conditions. It requires extended daylight and warm conditions that are more than 18 degrees Celsius at night can cause seeding. Water temperatures more than 26 degrees Celsius may also cause seeding and bitter leaves. Lettuce does not have a high nutrient demand, but it is advised that you increase calcium concentrations in your water in order to prevent the tips of the leaves from burning during summer months. The preferred pH is 5.8 to 6.2, but lettuce will still grow well with a pH level as high as 7, however, the lettuce could suffer from iron deficiencies at the higher pH levels. I would suggest that seedlings be transplanted to your Aquaponic set up around the three-week mark or when they are showing about 2 to 3 leaves. Adding phosphorus to the seedlings in the second and third weeks will aid in favorable root growth and help you to avoid stressing the plant when it is transplanted. Seedlings have an improved survival rate if they are exposed to colder temperatures direct sunlight for approximately 3 to 5 days prior to transplantation. On the contrary, when replanting in warm weather, light shade should be placed over the plants for two to three days beforehand to avoid water stress. If you maintain high nitrate levels, you should see faster growth rates as well as crisp, sweeter lettuce results.

- SWISS CHARD, also known as MANGOLD
    - pH levels are 6 to 7.5
    - Plant spacing requirements are 30 to 30 cm (15 to 20 plants/m$^2$)
    - Germination time and temperature will be 3 to 7 days at 25 to 30 degrees Celsius
    - Growth time is about 25 to 35 days
    - Temperature range is 16 to 24 degrees Celsius
    - Light exposure needed is full sun (partial shade for temperatures greater than 26 degrees Celsius)
    - Plant height and width will be 30 to 60 cm tall and 30 to 40 cm wide
    - Recommended Aquaponic method can be either media beds, NFT pipes or DWC

It is a very popular leafy green vegetable to grow using Aquaponics, because it does not require high levels of nitrate and requires very little potassium and phosphorous, it is ideally suited for Aquaponics growth. Swiss chard has a fast growth rate and high nutritional value. Though it is known as a leafy "green", it has amazing hints of yellow, purple and/ or red throughout its stem. Swiss chard is generally a late winter to spring vegetable however it prefers temperatures ranging between 16 and 24 degrees Celsius. Since it is a cool weather vegetable, it has the ability to survive temperatures as low as 5 degrees Celsius, yet it has also been known to fare well during mild summers. Swiss chard actually has a reasonable acceptance of salinity, which makes it an ideal plant for salt water. (This means it would be a great match for your Barramundi fish.) Swiss Chard is one of those leafy greens that allows us to remove larger leaves for use and leave the plant behind for the continued growth of new leaves.

Herbs: (We will highlight Basil and Parsley, to use for your guidelines to herbs)

- BASIL

- pH levels are 5.5 to 6.5
- Plant spacing requirements are 15 to 25 cm (8 to 40 plants/m$^2$)
- Germination time and temperatures are 6 to 7 days with temperatures at 20 to 25 degrees Celsius
- Growth time is about 5 to 6 weeks (harvest begins when the plant is about 15 cm)
- Temperature ranges are 18 to 30 degrees Celsius but are best at 20 to 25 degrees Celsius
- Light exposure needed is Sunny or lightly shaded
- Plant height and width will be 30 to 70 cm tall and 30 cm wide
- Recommended Aquaponic method can be either media beds, NFT or DWC uptake, however, it is important to avoid too much nutrient depletion in the water.

Basil seeds need a very high and constant temperature in order for germination to begin (20 to 25 degrees Celsius). After they have been transplanted to the media bed or desired set up, the basil will grow best in warm to very warm conditions and lots of sun with minimal shading for optimal leaves. If temperatures throughout the day exceed 27 degrees Celsius, the plants will need to be in a ventilated and or shaded area to prevent the tips of the leaves from burning. It is best to transplant new seedlings once they have 4 or 5 leaves. To avoid disease, stress, or mold, air ventilation is vital and water temperatures should be maintained above 21 degrees Celsius at all times. Once the plant is about 15 cm tall, you can harvest the leaves and continue to do so for 30 to 50 days. Make sure to leave a few flowering plants behind because they will attract beneficial insects that can improve the entire garden and help to keep a constant supply of basil seeds in production.

- PARSLEY
  - pH levels are 6 to 7
  - Plant spacing requirements are 15 to 30 cm (10 to 15 plants/m$^2$)
  - Germination time and temperature ranges are 8 to 10 days and 20 to 25 degrees Celsius
  - Growth time will be about 20 to 30 days after transplantation
  - Temperatures are 15 to 25 degrees Celsius

- Light exposure is full sun and partial shade when greater than 25 degrees Celsius
- Plant height and width are 30 to 60 cm tall and 30 to 40 cm wide
- Recommended aquaponic method can be either media beds, NFT or DWC

Parsley is a very common herb to grow due to its high levels of vitamins A and C, calcium and iron). Parsley is an easy herb to grow and has a low nutrient requirement. Parsley is a biennial herb, but it is traditionally grown as an annual. Highly resistant to temperatures as low as zero degrees Celsius but should not be exposed to temperatures lower than 8 degrees Celsius for optimal growth. Parsley needs full sunlight for up to eight hours a day. It should have partial shading if temperatures are greater than 25 degrees Celsius. Initial germination can take 2 to 5 weeks, depending on seeds freshness. Emerging seedlings will have the appearance of grass, with two narrow seed leaves opposite each other. After approximately 5 to 6 weeks you will be able to transplant the seedlings into your aquaponic setup. You can begin to harvest once the individual stalks of Parsley are at least 15 cm. If you harvest from the outside in, you will encourage growth production throughout the season. Many people remove the tops, but this will simply slow production.

Next, we will discuss tomatoes. Tomatoes have a complicated growth cycle and go through many changes during this time. There are two types of tomato plants amongst the variety of tomatoes. One type yields tomatoes all at one time and the other will yield tomato production periodically and continuously. This is important because if you choose the one that yields all at once, this species is a much smaller plant that doesn't need a support structure and can easily be grown indoors. The other species will vary in size dependent on the variety. Tomato plants require high humidity and prefer a temperature of 78 degrees Fahrenheit in order to yield fruit. Though this is their preference, tomatoes can yield fruit in temperatures ranging from 68 to 88 degrees Fahrenheit. It is important to maintain pH levels between 5.8 and 6.8 but can handle pH levels up 7.2. They require up to 12 hours of light per day and no less than 8 hours per day. The more light they get, the more fruit they will yield and the faster the plant will yield it. It is best to start from a cutting. If you start from seeds, you must have a separate seedling tray with a temperature at 77 degrees Fahrenheit and humidity at 100 percent. They will need to grow 2 to 6 weeks before transplanting them to the grow bed.

- TOMATO
    - pH levels are 5.5 to 6.5
    - Plant spacing requirements are 40 to 60 cm (3 to 5 plants/$m^2$)
    - Germination time and temperature are: 4 to 6 days in 20 to 30 degrees Celsius
    - Growth time will be 50 to 70 days till first harvest and fruiting 90 to 120 days upwards of 8 to 10 months (dependent on variety)
    - Optimal temperatures are 13 to 16 degrees Celsius at night, 22 to 26 degrees Celsius during daytime
    - Light exposure is full sun
    - Plant height and width will be 60 to 180 cm tall and 60 to 80 cm wide
    - Recommended Aquaponic method can be either media beds or DWC

Tomatoes are an excellent summer fruiting vegetable but they require structural support systems. It is important to consider the plant to fish ratios due to the high nutrient requirement of tomatoes. For proper growth, a high nitrogen concentration is needed during the early stages and potassium is needed during the flowering stage as well. Tomatoes enjoy warm temperatures with full sun exposure. If temperatures drop below 8 to 10 degrees Celsius, the plants will cease growth. Likewise, anything above 40 degrees Celsius can cause flowers to stop growing and the fruit to turn. Tomatoes have a moderate tolerance to salinity, which makes them suitable for areas where pure freshwater is not available. Higher saline levels during the fruiting stage can improve the quality of the tomato. Set stakes or plant support structures before transplanting to prevent root damage. You can transplant the seedlings at the 3 to 6-week mark, when the seedling is about 10 to 15 cm and when nighttime temperatures are consistently above 10 degrees Celsius. Once the plants reach a height of 60 cm, you need to determine whether you will continue the growth process as a bush or single stem, and you do so by pruning the unnecessary upper branches. Remove the leaves from the bottom 30 cm of the main stem for better air circulation and reduction of potential disease. Remove the leaves that are covering each fruit branch prior to ripening to aid in the proper flow of nutrition to the fruits and to accelerate growth.

Vegetables like cabbage, broccoli, cauliflower, radishes and kale all have similar preferences in the environment.

- CAULIFLOWER
    - pH levels are 6.0 to 6.5
    - Plant spacing requirements are 45 to 60 cm (3 to 5 plants/m$^2$)
    - Germination time and temperature are 4 to 7 days with temperature 8 to 20 degrees Celsius
    - Growth time is 2 to 3 months during spring and 3 to 4 months during autumn
    - Temperatures are 20 to 25 degrees Celsius for initial growth and 10 to 15 degrees Celsius for head setting in autumn
    - Light exposure is full sun
    - Plant height and width is 40 to 60 cm tall and 60 to 70 cm wide
    - Recommended Aquaponic method is media beds.

Cauliflower requires calcium for the production of heads. It is a very climate sensitive plant, therefore, selecting a suitable variety for your environment and ensuring proper timing for transplant is paramount for this plant to flourish. Preferred air temperature for the initial growth period of the plant is 15 to 25 degrees Celsius. Head formation requires colder temperatures of 10 to 15 degrees Celsius in autumn or 15 to 20 degrees Celsius in spring, as long as there is a good amount of humidity and full sun conditions. Cold temperatures are tolerated but there is a danger of frost damage. Also, light shade is good in warmer temperatures greater than 23 degrees Celsius. When plants are 3 to 5 weeks old and have 4 to 5 leaves, you can begin transplantation. Make sure they are placed about 50 cm apart. To keep the heads white, use string or rubber bands to keep the leaves covering it. When they reach about 6 to 10 cm in diameter, the harvest may take less than a week in ideal temperatures or as long as a month in cooler conditions. Harvest when the heads are compact, white and firm. Cauliflower is susceptible to pests, so it is important to incorporate some sort of pest control.

- HEAD CABBAGE
    - pH level is 6 to 7.2
    - Plant spacing requirements are 60 to 80 cm (4 to 8 plants/m$^2$)
    - Germination time and the temperature is 4 to 7 days with 8 to 29 degrees Celsius
    - Growth time will be 45 to 70 days from transplanting (dependent on variety and climate)
    - The preferred temperature is 15 to 20 degrees Celsius (growth ceases greater than 25 degrees Celsius)
    - Light exposure is full sun
    - Plant height and width is 30 to 60 cm high and 30 to 60 cm wide
    - Recommended Aquaponic method is media beds

Cabbage is a winter crop with preferred growing temperatures of about 15 to 20 degrees Celsius. It is important to harvest the cabbage prior to daytime temperatures reaching 23 to 25 degrees Celsius. When the heads begin to grow, it is vital that they have high concentrations of phosphorus and potassium. You will want to transplant seedlings when there are about 4 to 6 leaves and are at a height of 15 cm. Start harvesting when cabbage heads are firm and about 10 to 15 cm in diameter depending on the variety grown.

- BROCCOLI
    - pH levels are 6 to 7
    - Plant spacing requirements are 40 to 70 cm (3 to 5 plants/m$^2$)
    - Germination time and the temperature is 4 to 6 days with 25 degrees Celsius
    - Growth time will be 60 to 100 days from transplantation
    - Average daily temperature preferred is 13 to 18 degrees Celsius
    - Light exposure is full sun. It can tolerate partial shade but will mature slowly.
    - Plant height and width is 30 to 60 cm tall and 30 to 60 cm wide

- Recommended Aquaponic method is media beds

Broccoli growth is optimal when daytime temperatures are 14 to 17 degrees Celsius. Winter varieties require temperatures of 10 to 15 degrees Celsius for head formation. Broccoli can withstand higher temperatures if a higher humidity is present. Hot temperatures cause premature seeding. You can transplant seedlings into media beds once 4 to 5 leaves are visible and the plants are 15 to 20 cm tall. Seedlings need to be placed 40 to 50 cm apart. Broccoli is susceptible to pests so it is very important to maintain pest control methods. You can begin harvesting broccoli when the buds of the head are firm and tight.

Cucumbers, squash, and melons are vine crops and they have pretty much the same requirements for growth. These types of vegetables prefer temperatures ranging from 75 to 78 degrees Fahrenheit during the day and around 68 degrees Fahrenheit at night. Humidity levels must be no greater than 75 percent. They can take anywhere from 1 ½ to 2 months for full growth from seeds. There are many squash varieties such as summer squash like zucchini and yellow squash and the numerous winter squash like butternut, spaghetti, and acorn. Assorted melons include watermelon, cantaloupe, and honeydew.

- CUCUMBERS
  - pH levels are 5.5 to 6.5
  - Plant spacing requirements are 30 to 60 cm (depending on variety; 2 to 5 plants/m$^2$)
  - Germination time and the temperature is 3 to7 days with 20 to 30 degrees Celsius
  - Growth time is 55 to 65 days
  - Temperature is 22 to 28 degrees Celsius during the daytime, 18 to 20 degrees Celsius nightly; highly susceptible to frost.
  - Light exposure is full sun
  - Plant height and width is 20 to 200 cm tall and 20 to 80 cm wide
  - Recommended Aquaponic methods are media beds and DWC

Cucumbers, as well as squash, zucchini, and melons, are great summer vegetables. They are ideally suited to grow in media beds because they have a large root structure. Cucumbers can also be grown on floating rafts, but if you choose this method it is important to constantly check to grow pipes because there could be the risk of clogging from excessive root growth. Cucumbers require large quantities of nitrogen and potassium, so it is important to ensure proper plant to fish ratios. Cucumbers grow best with high humidity, lots of sunshine, and warm nights. They enjoy growth temperatures of 24 to 27 degrees Celsius during the daytime with 70 to 90 percent humidity. Plants cease growth and production at 10 to 13 degrees Celsius. Higher potassium concentration is preferred for higher fruit settings and yields. Cucumber seedlings can be transplanted at 2 to 3 weeks when there are 4 to 5 leaves showing. They grow very quickly. For optimal health of the fruit, you should cut their apical tips when the stem is two meters long, allowing more nutrient flow to the fruit. Remove the lateral branches to allow for enhanced ventilation. It is important to have beneficial insects around your cucumbers. It is also important to provide a support system for their growth and prevention of diseases and/ or molds. Once transplanted, cucumbers can start production in about 2 to 3 weeks. The plants can be harvested in ideal conditions 10 to 15 times. Make sure to harvest every few days to prevent the fruits from excessive growth and to promote new growth.

- EGGPLANT
    - pH level is 5.5 to 7.0
    - Plant spacing requirements are 40 to 60 cm (3 to 5 plants/m$^2$)
    - Germination time and the temperature is 8 to 10 days with 25 to 30 degrees Celsius
    - Growth time will be 90 to 120 days
    - Temperatures preferred are 15 to 18 degrees Celsius at night and 22 to 26 degrees Celsius during the day; highly susceptible to frost
    - Light exposure is full sun
    - Plant height and width is 60 to 120 cm tall and 60 to 80 cm wide
    - Recommended Aquaponic method is media beds

Eggplant is a summer fruiting vegetable that grows well in media beds because of their deep root system growth. These plants can produce 10 to 15 fruits for a total yield of 3 to 7 kg. Eggplants have high nitrogen and potassium requirements. Because of this, it is important to ensure a proper balance throughout the ecosystem. Eggplants enjoy warm temperatures with full exposure to sunlight. They grow best with daily temperatures in the range of 22 to 26 degrees Celsius and humidity of 60 to 70 percent. Temperatures less than 9 to 10 degrees Celsius and more than 30 to 32 degrees Celsius can cause growth and production cessation. Seeds germinate in 8 to 10 days in warm temperatures ranging between 26 to 30 degrees Celsius. Seedlings can be transplanted when 4 to 5 leaves are showing. Near the end of the summer, start pinching off new blooms to promote the ripening of any existing fruit. Towards the end of the season, plants can be pruned at 20–30 cm, leaving just three branches for the following season. This will stop any further growth until favorable seasons return. Start harvesting when the eggplants are 10–15 cm long. The skin should be shiny and deep purple.

- BEANS AND PEAS
    - pH level is 5.5 to 7.0
    - Plant spacing requirements are 10 to 30 cm dependent on variety (bush varieties 20 to40 plants/m$^2$, climbing varieties 10 to 12 plants/m$^2$)
    - Germination time and the temperature is 8 to 10 days with 21 to 26 degrees Celsius
    - Growth time is 50 to 110 days to reach maturity depending on the variety
    - Temperature is 16 to 18 degrees Celsius nightly, 22 to 26 degrees Celsius daytime
    - Light exposure is full sun
    - Plant height and width is 60 to 250 cm (climbing) and 60 to 80 cm (bush)
    - Recommended Aquaponic method is media bed

Beans have low nitrate needs but have a moderate demand in terms of phosphorus and potassium. Beans are recommended for newly established units as they may fix atmospheric nitrogen for you. Climbing varieties prefer full sunlight but will tolerate partial shade in warm conditions. Bean plants do not grow in temperatures lower than 12 to 14 degrees Celsius. Temperatures greater than 35 degrees Celsius can cause flower and fruit growth cessation. They enjoy humidity of 70 to 80 percent. It is important to choose the right varieties according to the location and season. In general, climbing varieties are cultivated in summer while others are better suited for spring and autumn conditions. Beans are susceptible to aphids and spider mites. It is a good idea to employ regular pest control procedures and attention needs to be paid as to which companion plants are placed in the garden in an effort to avoid cross-contamination in case any treatment has to be carried out. Snap bean varieties such as green or yellow wax beans have pods that need to be firm and crisp at harvest. Try to avoid pulling off branches that can offer future pods when pulling off the pods you are harvesting currently. Make sure to pick all pods off in order to keep plants productive. Shell beans such as black, broad or fava beans should be picked when the pods change color and the beans inside are fully formed but not dried out. Pods should be plump and firm. Dried beans such as kidney beans and soybeans need to become as dry as possible before cooler weather sets in or when plants have turned brown and lost most of their leaves. These pods will easily open when very dry, making seed removal a simple procedure.

- PEPPERS
    - pH level is 5.5 to 6.5
    - Plant spacing requirements are 30 to 60 cm (3 to 4 plants/m$^2$, or more for small-sized plant varieties)
    - Germination time and the temperature is 8 to 12 days with 22 to 30 degrees Celsius (seeds will not germinate at a temperature lower than 13 degrees Celsius)
    - Growth time is 60 to 95 days
    - Temperature is 14 to 16 degrees Celsius at night time, 22 to 30 degrees Celsius during the daytime
    - Light exposure is full sun
    - Plant height and width is 30 to 90 cm tall and 30 to 80 cm wide
    - Recommended Aquaponics method is media beds

There are numerous varieties of peppers with numerous assortments of color and varying degrees of Scoville levels (heat index). Regardless whether they are sweet bell pepper, hot chili peppers (jalapeño or cayenne peppers), or anything in between, they can all be grown in your Aquaponics garden. Peppers are best grown with the media bed system though they can also grow in

cm diameter NFT pipes if they have a good structural support system. Peppers are a summer fruiting vegetable that prefers warm conditions and full exposure to sunlight. Seeds germinate in temperatures at about 22 to 34 degrees Celsius. They cannot germinate well in temperatures below 15 degrees Celsius. Best conditions for fruiting are daytime temperatures of 22 to 28 degrees Celsius and night-time temperatures of 14 to 16 degrees Celsius. They also enjoy humidity of 60 to 65 percent. The best temperatures for the root levels are 15 to 20 degrees Celsius. Air temperatures below 10 to 12 degrees Celsius will cause plant growth cessation and additionally cause abnormally formed fruits. Temperatures that are higher than 30 to 35 degrees Celsius can lead to problems with the flowers and even cause them to fall off. Basically, peppers that are spicier can be grown at higher temperatures. The top leaves of the plant protect the fruit that is hanging below from getting sun exposure. As with other fruiting plants, nitrate is vital for the initial growth process. The best range of nitrate levels needed is 20–120 mg/liter but higher concentrations of potassium and phosphorus are needed for flowering and fruiting. Seeds should be transplanted when the plant shows 6 to 8 leaves and the night temperatures remain constant above 10 degrees Celsius. A strong structural support system is needed for bushy, heavy-yielding plants. Stakes or vertical strings hanging from iron wires pulled horizontally above the units should anchor them properly. If growing red sweet peppers, you need to leave the green fruits on the plants until they ripen and turn red. In order to encourage future plant growth, you should pick the first couple of flowers that make their appearance on the plant. Should excessive fruit setting occur, you will need to reduce the number of flowers on the plant. This will aid in promoting the growth of fruit to adequate sizes. You should begin harvesting when peppers reach appropriate sizes. Peppers need to be left on the plants until they ripen fully. You will recognize this by the change in color. Harvesting them at their optimal ripeness will improve their levels of vitamin C. If you harvest regularly throughout the season, your plants will continue to blossom fruit and promote growth. Peppers can be easily stored fresh for 10 days at 10 degrees Celsius with
90 to 95 percent humidity or they can be dehydrated or pickled for long-term storage.

**Ornamental fish for Aquaponics Fish Tanks:**

Some people simply want to reap the benefits of the Aquaponics system for Vegan consumption and enjoy the beauty of the fish that aid in the growth of their vegetables and herbs. Others too, want a purely ornamental set up for their home and are not concerned with food production at all. In either case, there are many fish to choose from. It is important to keep in mind the needs of the ecosystem as a whole to determine the size of the fish and/ or the amount of fish that you need in order to maintain proper balance throughout. Here are some suggestions for ornamental fish for the indoor tank:

- Angelfish are also known as the Koi Angel and come in many types and colors. Generally, they will be approximately six inches in size, therefore, a 20-gallon tank would be the minimum suggested and of course, is dependent on the amount of fish you desire.
- Goldfish tends to be the staple for home aquariums. These fish also come in many varieties differing in color, size, and shape. They are very durable fish so they can handle any size tank and do not require heat. They pretty much eat anything as they are not very picky eaters so the variety of foods and plants to choose from for their consumption are countless. Goldfish produce a large amount of waste for such a small fish, which actually makes them great for Aquaponics garden to grow. Because they tend to be shy, it is important to have plants in the tank itself for some type of retreat for the fish. The ideal water temperatures for Goldfish would be between 68 and 75 degrees Fahrenheit.
- Bloodfin Tetras are also very hardy fish that can withstand almost any environment. They are very beautiful with silver and red hues and therefore make for an attractive setup.
- The White Cloud Mountain Minnow is a small pretty fish well suited for the indoor aquarium as well as the outdoor pond! They do well with cold water conditions.
- Danios are also a small fish that are very durable fish that do well in almost any environment. They have beautiful

striped features and bright colors that look amazing as they race around your tank, traveling in schools. These fish will come to greet you at the top of the water when you feed them their flakes so you may enjoy a setup that has the plants placed on one side while the water is exposed for feeding on the other.

Note: In colder areas, heaters may be warranted to ensure that the water does not get too cold. The same would be the case for extremely hot areas where
the temperatures can reach into the three digits. It is important to maintain regular temperature ranges and not have the fish experience drastic fluctuations to stress them out, no matter how durable the species may be. Temperatures should never fluctuate more than three degrees!

For those of you who would like to enjoy outdoor ponds using Aquaponics, Koi are no doubt the most popular choice. These fish are not just beautiful and come in assorted colors, but they are omnivorous, parasite-resistant and thus live very long life spans upwards of 60 years. They produce an abundant amount of waste so they are great at helping the plants in and around your pond grow large and fast. One thing to keep in mind about Koi, they are easy to find for purchasing however they are very expensive fish to buy. Due to their durability, unbelievable beauty, and long life, the cost may very well be worth it! How many fish can you honestly say with certainty (in the ornamental category) will live a good amount of time or even survive when you make your purchase. Aside from making my pond area bear proof where I live, I am fairly certain that my investment in Koi is a good one that I will enjoy for years to come! (They may very well be there for the next generation after me to enjoy!)

**Edible varieties of fish for your Aquaponics system**
Obviously, there are many freshwater fish to choose from so I am just going to cover a select few that tend to be the top choices for Aquaponics. You can use this guide to deviate from this list as many fish are related in one way or another (like the Carp, Goldfish, and Koi, for example).

- Tilapia seems to be the number one choice amongst Aquaponics growers. This is understandable because Tilapia are easy to breed and are fast growing fish that are basically ready to be on your plate within 6 to 9 months. They are a warm water breed that enjoys temperature ranges between 72 and 86 degrees Fahrenheit. Aside from their ease of breeding and fast growth, they are delicious with a mild flavor that is used in many cuisines in various culinary styles. These fish are durable and can adapt to many less desirable environments though they, like everyone else, have their preference, and it is very important to maintain constant warm water temperatures if you want to keep your fish healthy, breeding, and growing at a consistent pace. These fish are omnivorous and can be placed in tanks with other species without concern of them eating the other fish. It is important to note that Tilapia breed rapidly (about every four to six weeks) so you must have a tank large enough to contain all the new schools.

- Trout is another option however it is important to recognize that they must be closely monitored due to their high Dissolved Oxygen levels and pH balance. Anything that throws their environment out of whack can be detrimental. They are cold water fish that enjoy temperature ranges between 56 and 68 degrees Fahrenheit. Trout can be ready for eating in 12 to 16 months though it is a more delicate fish than the warm water Tilapia, Trout is a great source of protein and Omega fatty acids and it is a delicious fish option. In reference to the marriage in this ecosystem, the options for your plants are reduced because of the colder water requirements, therefore it is important if choosing this fish that you also choose plants that are very hardy and can withstand cooler water temperatures.

- Perch is a highly adaptable fish that comes in a variety of silver, yellow and jade. Because of their adaptability, they have been a good option for the beginner Aquaponics growers. They can handle cooler water temperatures but their ideal temperature range would be between 70 and 82 degrees Fahrenheit. Depending on which variety of Perch you choose, you can be eating your Perch as early as 9 months or in the case of the silver Perch, up to 16 months. Perch are carnivorous fish so you need to feed them smaller fish, bugs, and shrimp. This may be a more expensive diet for your fish but the taste of Perch is worth it for those who can afford the additional expense.

- Catfish have become very popular options for Aquaponics because they grow extremely fast allowing the breeder to enjoy the taste of this delectable fish in only 5 to 10 months. Catfish are sensitive to water temperature, water quality, and pH like the Trout, so there is a need to be diligent with maintaining a pristine environment. They require temperature ranges between 78 and 86 degrees Fahrenheit. Catfish are bottom dwellers that come in many sizes. This fish offers great flavor and are high in vitamin D, which most people tend to be deficient in. One thing to note about catfish is that they do not have scales, so it is important to skin the fish before you prepare it for consumption.

- Barramundi is a special option, in that this fish, unlike the others, can be kept in both freshwater systems and saltwater systems. (Pleases note: Saltwater is not recommended for Aquaponics simply because of the lack of plant options available for your system.) Barramundi must not be kept with small fish because they will get very aggressive and can injure or even eat the younger smaller fish. This is a white fish that is very flaky and tasty, thus the reason for its popularity. They grow rather quickly and can be on your plate within 12 months time. These fish do require perfect water conditions and therefore need to be monitored regularly. Dissolved Oxygen levels need to be regulated. That being said, they are great fish to watch in your tank and they have a high waste output for a thriving garden.

- Largemouth, smallmouth, and striped Bass are very popular Aquaponics fish as well. They prefer a temperature range between 75 and 85 degrees Fahrenheit. Dependent on the type you choose, it will be fully matured for serving in 12 to 18 months, with Striped Bass growing quicker. They require pristine water conditions, dark areas (they do not like bright lights), they need proper oxygen and pH levels and must follow a strict feeding schedule. Bass is a very delicious source of food and like Tilapia, has been used in many culinary forms and cuisines, so the recipes are numerous.

- It's funny but most people don't think about Crustaceans when deciding to do Aquaponics, however they are gaining in popularity the more Aquaponics becomes known around the world. Thinking outside the "fish" box (or tank, I should say, lol), Crustaceans offer great variety for your meals and are definitely a viable choice in Aquaponics systems. The best part is that many fish can cohabitate with your crustaceans! Setting the carnivores aside, you can place Mussels, Oysters, Crayfish, freshwater prawns, shrimp, crabs, and even lobster, in your tank. Aside from a food source for us humans, they are great at keeping the tank clean because they tend to eat dead organic plant matter. Many people tend to keep a separate tank for their crustaceans if they are planning on using them for human food as opposed to fish food. Even if your fish won't eat them, many may decide to attack them, and just like fish, we want to keep them healthy and stress-free. Mussels are a bit different than the others in this category because they can grow in the tank as well as in the grow beds! For your prawns, they prefer temperature ranges between 82 and 88 degrees Fahrenheit and can be served within 6 to 12 months. Your lobster prefers 71 to 76 degrees Fahrenheit and can be served in 24 months. The oysters enjoy temperatures of 75 to 79 degrees Fahrenheit and can be on your plate in 24 months.

Special Mention: The past few years, we hear about cannabis in the news either about the medical breakthroughs they are reporting in terms of benefits in the fight against cancer, Alzheimer's, PTSD, seizures and other ailments or about how state after state is approving the legalization of cannabis. With that being said, I thought I would briefly mention that Aquaponics is also an area in which Cannabis growth has seen great success. Since we are discussing plants, there may be a few of you interested in attempting this. Though it is not new to Hydroponics, it is newer to Aquaponics but there are plenty of articles online and books on this subject if you should be interested in doing so and they discuss legal allowances for different regions as well as proper set up conducive to growth for these particular plants.

# CHAPTER 4

## *How to Create A Proper Aquaponics Environment*

You now have a good idea of what you would like your Aquaponics garden to look like and where it will be located. You know what kind of plants you want in your garden and what kind of fish you would like in your tank. The next step is to choose the system you feel would work best for you and work on all of the factors that are required to ensure that your Aquaponics ecosystem will function properly and allow your plants and fish to thrive.

## TYPES OF SYSTEMS

**Sun Pond**
The basic set up is reminiscent of that used by the Aztecs. It simply consists of the plants floating directly on the pond or tank water with its roots submerged in the water. The biggest issue with this design arises with the inability to stop fish from eating and damaging the plants.

**Flood and Drain**
This is the most common of the Aquaponics systems, due to its simplicity. An even ratio of fish tank volume to plant bed volume makes for an easy calculation. The system utilizes three components: the fish tank, the pump, and the grow bed. Water is pumped directly from the fish tank to the media bed. The media bed then drains back into the fish tank. It's the circle of life! This works best with a single bed area. Having two or more can lead to low water levels and stress on the fish.

**CHOP**
The acronym CHOP stands for constant height, one pump. This system is like the flood and drain except that there is the addition of the sump pump in order to maintain the water levels at a consistent height. The pump is located in a separate sump tank. The water from the fish tank overflows into the grow beds. The grow beds then drain into the sump tank which then pumps the water back to the fish tank.

This system is less stressful on the fish because of the water level maintenance but does require a lot more space and can present difficulties with supply needs. The set up for this system requires that the sump tank area is lower than the grow bed area which also needs to be lower than the fish tank.

## CHOP 2

This system obviously is very much like the CHOP except the way that it is set up is very different. The CHOP has a more vertical relation to each part where the CHOP2 is horizontal in relation to where its life producing tanks are located. This system requires that the fish tank and the media beds sit level with each other with the only part sitting below them being the sump tank area. The sump tank pumps water to the media beds and the fish tank. The grow beds utilize an auto siphon to receive their much-needed water and the fish tank utilizes a gravity feed overflow mechanism. With this system, you can have two or more grow bed areas feeding off of the one fish tank. Doing so would require a larger setup and stronger pumping mechanisms. Because the sump tank doubles its duty, clean and dirty water mixes and filtration is not efficient. Additional filtration would be recommended in order to reach an optimal ecosystem environment.

## AUTOMATION

There are so many things that go on in our day to day lives. If we could make one part of it that much easier and not have to think about it constantly, why wouldn't you?

An Aquaponics system can be run seamlessly on an automated system. Our ancestors did not have this luxury and had to maintain a rigorous schedule to ensure that they fed the fish, the water quality was tested, the temperature was as it should be, the filter was clear of any solid waste obstructions, and pumping mechanisms were doing their job.

These days, everything can be done by machines and computers and can even be monitored on smart devices from remote locations far away from the Aquaponics site. Sensors that are computer monitored don't have to be astronomically priced as they come in a range of prices and capacities. They are made to alert you when something in your system is not quite right and depends on what the problem is, they can automatically correct the problem. Not everyone is up to this technology. It does require some programming/setting. I still need help using my I-phone. Thank God for my kids. It's amazing what they know about technology even before they are teenagers.

For me, more simple systems of automation like timers work just fine, especially when you are using a flood and drain system. A timer must be set up to control the system as they use settings to cause the flood and drain to occur. The time is usually set for every hour on the hour for 15 minutes in duration, in an effort to fill the media beds. During the remaining 45 minutes of the hour, the media beds are draining into the fish tank.

For others, an auto siphon, also known as a bell siphon, is preferred. This method remains active at all times because it works through the use of an overflow spout. Once the water level rises causing overflow, the siphon automatically opens and releases the water from the media beds into the fish tank. Once the media bed is drained, the siphon closes again and waits to refill. The process will continue automatically unless a solid is caught in the siphon, causing a blockage.

If you are still interested in some type of automation at a budget but want something a bit more sophisticated, you might want to look into APDuino. APDuino is a firmware that is specifically designed for both Aquaponic and Hydroponic systems and can be set through wi-fi or hard-wired. There are others out there, so it is recommended that you do your research to see what best meets your needs and your budget.

Even for those who have been enjoying the relaxation of owning an aquarium, automatic feeders have become popular, especially for those with an assortment of fish with differing feeding needs. This is a great option for Aquaponics.

Aside from monitoring and repairing, automated systems have been beneficial in mimicking day and night. Shading and venting can be incorporated to ensure that the system is temperature regulated. The shade will minimize the heat produced from the sun and the vent will cool the garden by releasing the hot air that has accumulated. This, of course, is not a necessity since it is not difficult to open and close curtains and windows, however, if you are not near your Aquaponics garden for long periods of time (most people spend more time at work then they do at home) then this luxury doesn't sound so ridiculous, does it? Finding the right location for your garden that will allow for a good balance, may help to avoid the added expenditure.

Automatic lighting is another feature to consider indoors or out. It is important to have sunlight, but we don't always have sunny days and of course, when we do, it doesn't stay as day must go and night must come. Lighting doesn't just affect how much "sunlight" a plant gets but also the temperature the garden experiences. We will discuss lighting and temperatures in more detail later on in the chapter.

## BIOFILTRATION

Biofilters are made to duplicate the processes naturally occurring in nature. Aquaponics incorporates biofilters to ensure that it mimics mother nature's work as closely as humanly possible. Aquaponics systems make sure that no waste occurs as everything is vitally important just as it is in nature. Saying that, recycle and reuse is not just something we say but something we must do. Aquaponics does just that since the excreta from the fish is used as a source of food for the garden and, just like any natural ecosystem, one hand washes the other, so the plants will clean the water for the fish. In the next chapter, we will discuss in detail the nutrient cycle, but biofilters are a part of that necessary cycle. The medium which facilitates the nutrient cycle is called a biofilter. Regular aquariums require extensive filtration systems to achieve a healthy environment but with planted aquariums like in Aquaponics, the plants act as a natural biofilter, so the filtration needed is much less extensive and more inexpensive. In fact, in using the flood and drain method with media beds, added filtration is not needed. The plants in the Aquaponic garden remove all the nitrites and nitrates that are harmful to fish but stimulate growth in plants. If fish to plant bed ratios are properly calculated, biofiltration can simply be done by the plants. For the most part, in Aquaponics, this is the case. Sometimes the plants need a bit of help so additional filtration can be incorporated. This may occur in a DWC configured grow bed, but it is not likely needed with media beds.

**TANKS**
Depending on the type of system you choose, you may not only need a tank for your fish but a tank for your sump pump as well. Some people will additionally purchase a tank to grow fingerlings until they are big enough to survive in a tank with adult fish who might like to make a meal out of them. Generally, I like to keep one or the other so one tank would suffice.

It is important to keep in mind that aquariums are made for fish. Aquaponics gardens are made for plants and fish, edible fish mostly, and for that reason, the two don't automatically go together. Aquariums are chemically treated and require filtration systems to ensure that the water is not toxic to the fish who inhabit it. The biofiltration of plants in such an environment without an additional filtration system will cause algae to build up. Algae are detrimental to both plants and fish because it sucks the oxygen from the water for their own needs.

Additionally, ornamental fish versus fish breeds used for consumption have different environmental needs. A well-lit aquarium setting for Guppies, Mollies, or other ornamental fish, even Koi in a pond, works great but fish like Tilapia and Bluegill tend to prefer darker areas with places to hide, especially when they feel danger looming (and that could simply be someone looking in the tank).

Purchasing a kit, as previously discussed. It will ensure that you have the proper set up for your plants and fish. If you choose the DO IT YOURSELF path and want an aquarium as part of your set up, the size must be considered to determine if biofiltration by the plants will be suitable or if an additional filtration system is needed. Aquariums are safe and watertight for marine inhabitants so if the worst thing you need to add to your DO IT YOURSELF project budget is a filtration system, it's worth it.

Other containment systems can be used like barrels, tanks, bathtubs, etc. but again, this would be covered extensively in a DO IT YOURSELF manual specific to Aquaponics. These alternate containment systems do require many more steps to ensure that there is no toxic residue and that the parts you choose for your system are food grade and/or drinking water safe. It is better to be safe than sorry, not just for the living organisms, plants, and fish in your Aquaponics ecosystem, but also for the people who intend to consume the plants and/or fish cultivated in the garden. So, therefore, DO IT YOURSELF people, when in doubt, don't use it, count it as out!!!

## GROW BEDS

The general depth for Aquaponics' grow beds is 12 inches as that is optimal for growth, biofiltration, and temperatures. If you intend to utilize Aquaponics systems for large plants and/or trees, then doubling the depth to 24 inches is advised. For most grow beds, 12 inches is perfect to allow room for the root system and its natural processes. Whether your garden utilizes media (which allows, at this depth, biofiltration, conversion of ammonia to nitrate, to occur) or is directly submerging the roots in water (having the roots this deep allows for stability in temperature), 12 inches in depth has proven to deliver conditions conducive to a flourishing Aquaponics ecosystem.

# TYPES OF GROW BEDS:

### Media Based

The most commonly used grow beds are those that use items like rocks or gravel for biofiltration. Media based refers to anything that is used to give a support system to the plants since they don't have the soil to do that function.

Media can include:

- Rocks
- Gravel
- Sand
- Perlite
- Styrofoam
- Mineral wood
- Clay beads

Mostly commonly used media:

- Gravel
- Expanded Shale
- Clay beads

The ideal size of the medium should be ¾ inches in diameter to allow for proper drainage from plant bed to fish tank.

Previously discussed in this book, it is important to consider weight when setting up your Aquaponics garden because it is not only the fish tank that has considerable weight (example: a 100 gallon fish tank weighs about 1150 pounds when filled with water) but the grow beds have a great amount of weight also, especially in those using media based beds.

The use of media in your beds allows for a broader selection of plants, trees, bushes, or root vegetables to be grown. Heavier, taller plants can be cultivated because of the support system that media-based beds offer.

Media based beds create ideal surfaces for mineralization to occur whereas water-based beds tend to be too diluted to allow the plants to gain the nourishment that they need. As the oxygenated water and excretions from the fish collect on the rocks (or whatever medium is chosen) in the bed, the natural cycle will begin to transform the chemical compounds into the nutrients plants so desperately need.

Another benefit of using media based beds is algae prevention. The media used like rocks block the light from hitting the roots of the plants whereas water-based systems do not have any natural shields. If the roots get attacked by algae, it impairs their ability to breathe, drink, and filter. Likewise, if the roots are exposed to direct light, they can get burnt and impair their ability to absorb water.

Also, an important function of media based beds, as mentioned earlier, is the filtration. Removing the media from the equation opens the doors for several issues. If waste is not removed from the fish tank, it is not only deadly to the fish but it can also cause blockage in the roots of the plants which will prevent them from eating and drinking. They need water and nutrients to survive. For both the fish and plants, water-based systems require added filtration systems whereas media based beds eliminate the need because of their natural biofiltration process.

As I've said earlier, I aim to find a happy balance between form and function. Media beds allow for creativity, beauty, and a harmoniously functioning ecosystem to happen all in the same place. Koi ponds are great examples of this. Koi ponds have been designed with Aquaponics systems and amazing elements of design using media beds. They have beautiful plants and trees surrounding the pond and some even have plants on the pond, which make for a hybrid design of sorts. Incorporating Lily pads or other floating plants are elements of water-based systems. Additionally, waterfalls aid in biofiltration and water movement throughout the system and rock placement creates a beautiful environment.

The design you choose can be a real statement piece indoors or out and media based systems make it easier to do so, whereas, the need for filtration in water-based systems can be a real eyesore.

Obviously, media-based beds have many positive attributes but there are a few negatives that need to be mentioned for the sake of allowing you to make fully informed decisions as to which system you prefer for your personal Aquaponics garden.
As noted before, weight is certainly a factor to consider. Water alone is heavy but the addition of media such as rocks will increase the weight requirements of the area you choose, significantly.

Secondly, just like any filter, media beds can get clogged, which will cause a lack of oxygen to travel to the plants and ultimately to the fish. There are several indicators that will let you know that there is a potential threat from clogging:

- Rapid increase in pH
- Reduction in water flow through the bed
- Dense balls of roots have formed

Third, if the media used in the beds are not pH neutral or hasn't been rinsed first, a simple item like dirt or sand on the media might throw the pH levels out of balance.

Fourth, media doesn't just vary in assorted options, but it also varies in weight and cost.

It is very common for Aquaponics enthusiasts to select media such as:
- Gravel
- River rock
- Clay pellets
- Expanded shale

As far as price and availability, gravel is the least expensive, easy to obtain, and is beautiful for the garden, however, it is the heaviest option. Additionally, edges can be jagged and sharp, making it difficult to clean and arrange in beds without the use of thick protective gloves. River rocks are a good alternative since they have smooth edges but they are just as heavy. They are ideal for the support of heavier, taller plants.

The clay pellets are extremely lightweight but are much more difficult to find which results in a much more expensive purchase. Shale is very lightweight, weighing in slightly more than clay, and looks just like gravel. Shale is also in high demand and therefore carries a much higher price tag.

It is important to note, regardless of whether you purchase lightweight or heavier medium, media based grow beds will still be considerably weighty.

It is also important to stick to the dimensions advised. Anything smaller than ¾ inches will clog your system. It defeats the intention of the media bed altogether.

**Water Based Grow Beds**
There are two major ways of growing in water using Aquaponics:

- **DWC** (Deep Water Culture)
- **NFT** (Nutrient Film Technique)

We have discussed the benefits and drawbacks of media based beds and now we are going to explore the water-based grow beds and their pros and cons of use in Aquaponics. Before we discuss the two major ways to grow in water (DWC and NFT), we will look at the basics of water-based gardens.

Water-based gardening can be placed in locations that the heavier media based gardens simply could not go due to their weight restrictions. Because the roots of your plants are submerged, or partially submerged in water, there is no need for flooding and draining, and aside from occasional evaporation, water levels should remain consistent.

Water-based systems will require that filtration systems be put in place to remove fish solids and maintain proper levels for fish and plants. Plants will need to be in specialized containers for proper support. Because a filter is incorporated into the process to remove fish solids from clogging the plant roots which will prevent oxygen and nutrient absorption, it is absolutely imperative that proper nutrient rich mixtures be added to the environment. Also, filters require cleaning to ensure that they continue to work properly. In addition to the filter, it is important to add an aeration system to ensure adequate oxygen levels are achieved.

## NFT
In Nutrient Film Technique, the plants will be handing over a water-filled container that the roots of the plant drop into in order to drink and eat. The water in these containers is shallow, as it is just enough for the roots to get what they need.

In an NFT system, it is important to maintain the same temperature for the water as you do for the growing area. Because of this, it is difficult to maintain these systems outdoors regardless of the season.

## DWC
In the Deep Water Culture system, the grow beds are flooded at all times. This system is much more productive than the NFT system. This system most closely resembles that of our ancestors, centuries

ago, as it is a raft-like system of floating the plant holders in deep water.

## PLUMBING
Utilizing a kit versus DO IT YOURSELF does not require any plumbing knowledge and techniques, however, DO IT YOURSELF plumbing requires much more skill and knowledge. Some things to keep in mind in DO IT YOURSELF and of course to be covered in an extensive DO IT YOURSELF manual, would be:

- Always be mindful of using products that are drinking water safe. If it says "non-potable", you cannot use it for the Aquaponics system. Did you know that garden hoses are not drinking water safe?
- Plumbing used to take water to the grow beds is often exposed to sunlight which can erode piping like PVC, which is the common piping choice due to its inexpensive cost.
- 90-degree angled piping will cause flow reduction and can have blockages occur due to water pressure and direction of flow.
- Be mindful of plumbing near electrical outlets. A leak could be extremely dangerous.
- Always keep in mind your plant and fish needs when developing your plumbing structures. Air and water are vital components and therefore the set up you choose for aeration, filtration, and water movement is of utmost importance to the life of the ecosystem you build.
- The entire amount of water in your system must be circulated hourly.
- An inexpensive way to ensure adequate oxygen supply is to have an air pump with a diffuser.

## WATER
Water makes the Aquaponics system go round. Literally, without water, the plants and fish could not survive. We cover some form of Biology in most of what we do in learning how to be successful in Aquaponics, but now it's time to discuss another area of science. Hold on and get onboard our time machine, we are going back to chemistry 101 class to get a brief review. I loved science, but Chemistry was not my favorite. However, now that we are delving into the world of Aquaponics and creating our own ecosystem, the

knowledge of basic chemistry becomes very important, especially when discussing water.

Without getting too heavy into chemical breakdowns and equations, this section will discuss the difference between acids, neutrals, and alkalis, so that we have a better understanding of pH balance.

Water ($H_2O$) is a compound made up of two Hydrogen atoms and one Oxygen atom. In water, Hydrogen ions and Hydroxide ions are of equal counts in Water and were formed when molecules divided up. Those molecules that lost a hydrogen become known as Hydroxide ions and that little hydrogen that left the molecule, connected with water molecules to make Hydrogen ions. Because there is an equal balance of the two types of ions, water is neutral.

Once this balance is thrown off in either direction, we get an acid or a base, also known as an alkaline. When a substance is dissolved in water, it will either become acidic or basic (alkaline). An acid will demonstrate a higher amount of Hydrogen ions than Hydroxide ions when dissolved in water. The opposite is true of alkalis. A base is a solution with more Hydroxide ions than Hydrogen ions when it is dissolved in water.

We measure acidity and alkalinity with a pH scale. What does this mean? A one unit value on the pH scale corresponds to a change in Hydrogen ions multiplied by 10 for each value change. Water sits on the center of the pH scale at a value of 7. Basically, anything registering a value lower than water on the pH scale is considered Acids and anything registering values higher than water on the pH scale are considered bases or alkaline.

So that you can get an idea of what might register a pH value of an acid or a base in comparison to water, I have listed some acids and alkaline you might be familiar with below:

**Acids**
- Battery Acid (pH= 0)
- Vinegar (pH= 2)
- Orange Juice (pH= 3)
- Black Coffee; Bananas (pH= 5)

- Milk (pH= 6)

**Alkalines**
- Eggs (pH= 8)
- Baking Soda (pH= 9)
- Milk of Magnesia (pH= 10)
- Soapy Water (pH= 12)
- Liquid Drano (pH= 14)

So why is this chemistry lesson so important? Both acids and bases can cause a lot of damage. Plants thrive in an environment that has a pH levels registering anywhere between a value of 6 or 7. Most people automatically think of acids as harmful substances, but bases contain a lot of salts and metals in them which can be highly corrosive. Distilled water is completely safe for your ecosystem as it is a neutral, pH value of 7. Due to the damaging effects that acids and bases can have on both your plants and your fish, and yes, even the plumbing and tank, it is extremely important that pH levels are tested regularly.

**Water Weight**

I use this excuse every time I get on the scale, but it is true, water weighs a lot! I mentioned this fact several times throughout the book so I will just touch upon this briefly here. Sometimes math can throw us for a loop, and like chemistry, math was not my favorite subject but it comes in handy in Aquaponics. Most people will automatically know how many gallons of water they may be able to fit in their tank or container but being aware of what each of those gallons weighs is very important. Did you know that one gallon of water is equivalent to eight pounds? Let's put those numbers in perspective. If you buy a 100-gallon tank to house your fish, this means that yes; it will hold 100 gallons of water. The tank full of water will then weigh approximately 1150 pounds! That is a major amount of weight and not every location can support this kind of weight and in Aquaponics gardens, water is not the only factor causing the scales to tip. Additionally, it is important to consider square footage in regards to weight. The dirt outside can actually withstand up to 200 pounds per square foot and a basement made of concrete flooring could withstand half that weight.

**Water Temperature**
The climate that your fish prefer plays an important role in their survival and growth. There are not many plants or fish that can adapt to varying habitats. Temperature is a key factor in ensuring an ideal environment for your ecosystem. Water, important to both fish and plants, is very sensitive to temperatures and can easily heat up or cool down due to intervention from an external source that comes in direct contact with it. Additionally, the plants and fish in your Aquaponic ecosystem need oxygen to thrive, and in fact, without it would perish. They get their oxygen from water. Did you know that temperature can affect the amount of oxygen that is dissolved in water and therefore how much oxygen the pants and fish are getting?

During warm days, as the sun beats down on your garden, everything is feeling the effects of the heat. You may not think about it, but the rocks hold a lot of heat, the plumbing holds in heat, and of course, the tank itself. When the water comes in contact with hot surfaces, it will absorb their heat, which will increase the temperature of the water. Maintaining specific temperature ranges for your plants and fish in the ecosystem you created, is vital for it to thrive. In order to do so, use a thermometer specifically designed to measure water temperatures. It is important to check this on a daily basis, and if possible, several times per day. For those that choose to automate, this is one of those areas that I would recommend having an automated monitor because it will alert you the moment the temperatures rise or drop out of proper range. Temperature fluctuations happen constantly throughout the course of a day, whether your garden is inside or out, it will feel those changes. Not all fluctuations will be enough to make a difference that will knock temperatures out of range, however, keeping an eye on this is very important. If you live in an area where you don't experience a change in seasons, it's a bit easier avoiding drastic temperature changes, but for those of us that do experience the four seasons, extra measures, pardon the pun, need to be taken. Here are some suggestions:

- Whether you are heading into the hot summer months or the freezing winter months, insulation is a great way to moderate temperatures. Keep in mind that there are different types of insulation. In order to keep the pipes from getting too much heat exposure, an insulation that has a reflective outer shield is recommended. Other types of insulation (without reflective shield) would work well to maintain normal temperatures and keep pipes from freezing. It is also suggested that tanks and/or containers have insulation if outdoors during the colder months and adding extra rocks (or other media) to your grow beds will help give them additional insulation.

- If your garden is outdoors and exposed to the elements of seasonal changes, it would help to put a temporary covering over the area, giving it a greenhouse effect.
- When water is moving, the energy produced is converted to heat and therefore will be less likely to freeze. To keep water movement constant, make sure to run your air pump at all times.
    - Maintaining a constant flow of water through the use of an air pump will additionally ensure that oxygen is circulating throughout your system.

**Evaporation and Condensation**

Warm, dry air attracts moisture and cold air repels it. When your tank water is exposed to the thirsty warm air, the air will start to drink from the tank. When the water disappears from the tank into the air it is called evaporation. Differences in temperatures can react in other ways. If the air is colder than your garden, it will cause moisture from the air to be released and build upon area surfaces outside of your garden like perhaps a window. If your garden is cooler than the air, this effect known as condensation will occur right in your garden. Remember, it is important to maintain balance in the ecosystem you create, so both conditions should be avoided as they can affect temperature fluctuations as well as dissolved oxygen levels. I will discuss dissolved oxygen shortly but first, let's discuss ways in which you can deal with evaporation and condensation.

- Having a thermometer that measures the humidity is a good start.

- Try to reduce how much water is exposed to the air. Placing a cover over the tank or container would help minimize exposure.
- You can cover areas of water in the grow beds as well by simply adding an additional couple of inches of media.

The amount of natural evaporation that occurs in the Aquaponics garden will only be about 1/10 of the amount that would occur in a soil grown garden so top off your tank water to maintain optimal water levels. Remember, you never have to replace the water in Aquaponics because doing so would waste all the natural nutrients produced in that water.

**Dissolved Oxygen**
The water temperature has a profound effect on the activity and behavior of fish. It also affects their feeding habits, growth rates, and reproduction. As I mentioned earlier, water temperatures affect oxygen levels, which are not just important to fish but are also important to the plants and bacteria in your Aquaponic ecosystem. In order for aquatic creatures to get the oxygen they need, it must be dissolved in water. When those dissolved oxygen levels are lower than a reading of 5, fish in your garden will become stressed. The closer that reading comes to 2 and the longer it remains in that vicinity, stress is increased and the death of the fish will be imminent.

How do temperatures affect the dissolved oxygen levels? Warmer temperatures of water are saturated by oxygen and as a result, can hold less oxygen; therefore, the dissolved oxygen levels are lower. Colder temperatures of water are the opposite; therefore, the dissolved oxygen levels are higher. This conversation always reminds me of the three little bears and Goldilocks. One is too hot. One is too cold. Well, the fish want it "just right" also. Let's look at dissolved oxygen and temperature another way. In warmer water environments, fish metabolism speeds up, so the fish require more oxygen, but warmer water has low dissolved oxygen levels. As you can imagine, if the fish are desperately in need of oxygen, they begin to get erratic, kind of like someone who is drowning, they act panicked. In colder water environments, the metabolism of the fish slows down, so they need less oxygen, however, cold water has a higher level of dissolved oxygen. The high levels cause the fish to be tired and sleepy, which affects feeding habits and reproduction.

If your levels are low, in addition to monitoring and controlling temperatures to avoid issues with oxygen levels, using an aeration system will help to add oxygen to both the fish tank and the grow beds. When levels are high, it may be time to add more grow beds since the plants share the oxygenated water with the fish.

Adding plants mean more life using the oxygen and thus dissolved oxygen levels should decrease. Aside from your oxygen monitors reflecting a change in oxygen levels, you should see a change in behavior of your aquatic species.

## Light
Light is essential to the well being of plants and for that reason, just as it is important to know about water, temperature, nutrients, and oxygen (vital knowledge to have in order to maintain a thriving ecosystem), it is equally important to understand the many facets of light, the difference in light sources, and how these variables affect life in your Aquaponics garden.

There is obviously a big difference between growing indoors and outdoors when it comes to light, and though there are natural advantages of the sun's light outdoors, there are still things that need to be taken into consideration when growing outside. This section will discuss proper lighting for both indoor Aquaponics and outdoor Aquaponics gardening.

Plants have a molecule called Chlorophyll which takes light and changes it into energy that the plants can absorb. Because the plants feed off the energy produced by light to grow, having the proper lighting is a must for them to thrive. Different plants require different amounts of light (called lumens) and different plants respond to different colors of light (called wavelengths).

## Amount
First, it is important to recognize that the light people process with their eyes to see, is very different from the light plants need to process for their energy requirements. The wavelengths plants use are red and/or blue and are known as photosynthetically active

radiation referred to by its acronym PAR. To figure out the optimal PAR quantity for your indoor garden plants, you must consider four things:

- Distance of light to plants
- Type of bulb
- Type of light fixture
- Amount of natural light present

If your garden is outside in direct sunlight, it is receiving 100,000 lux (lumens per square meter). Not all plants thrive in direct sun exposure like a cactus. Most plants require 20,000 lux which is what they would get on a day with normal clear conditions. Regular indoor lights found in a kitchen or office, may produce 400 lux. These differences alone explain why proper lighting conditions are so important. In an Aquaponics garden, a variety of plants can be grown at the same time and though you may have all warm weather plants or all cold climate plants, requiring the same temperatures and lighting, the height of the plants can also make a difference. A tall plant in the wrong location may block light from getting to some of the shorter plants. Because Aquaponics uses grow beds versus soil, you can easily rearrange the plants in your garden to ensure they all get the light they need.

Artificial lighting known as grow lights are a serious blessing but there are so many options out there and the price is not the only factor to consider. Dependent on the amount of area you need to light and which bulbs that you use, you will need to figure out how many of that particular bulb it will take to release the sufficient amount of energy the plants in your garden require. For example, if you have a 16 sq ft area garden, you would need only one high-intensity discharge HPS bulb of 400 watts. But if you chose to use fluorescent light bulbs, you would need five of the 125 watt compact to grow lights, ten of the high output 54 watt lights, or forty-two of the 40 watt standard fluorescent lights. You would need twice as many standard white 60 watt light bulbs than standard fluorescent.

Obviously, you would probably vote for buying and using fewer bulbs but you also need to consider price and how often you would need to replace them. Though fluorescent lighting requires more bulbs, the lighting fixture and the bulbs are relatively inexpensive, energy efficient, and take up a smaller amount of space. The issue is that they need to be replaced after only six months in order to get proper PAR for your garden. Also, fluorescents are not a highly effective PAR for denser gardens.

High-intensity discharge bulbs work the best and most closely resemble the light given off by the sun, however, it is expensive and so are the fixtures. Additionally, they are energy intensive and emit a lot of heat.

# CHAPTER 5
## *Nutrient Cycle & Bacteria*

Well, if you thought your science lesson was over, you were definitely mistaken. Chemistry 101 continues as we delve deeper into Aquaponics. It is time to learn about a major part of the circle of life in our Aquaponics system. Many seem to forget about this process and how it works when they attempt to simply define how exactly Aquaponics works. I imagine the same is true for how cow manure fertilizes the crops. How many people have actually thought about how and why manure actually helps the crops grow? I know I never gave it a second thought. I just knew it worked. Well, in Aquaponics it is extremely important to know how to fish poop feeds your plants. Because we are essentially creating an ecosystem, for the ecosystem to function like a natural ecosystem, we have to help it out and play "mother nature" in our garden. How can we help our fish to help our plants to help our fish? Well, Mother Nature does her job so efficiently that we don't think a lot about the inner workings and intricacies behind nature and how it is able to thrive. Hopefully, by the time you are done with not just this chapter, but this book, you will have a much better grasp and ability to help nature take its course in the Aquaponics ecosystem you create.

## Ammonia, Nitrites, and Nitrates

Nitrogen is extremely important to the life of plants and through nitrogen is found in the air we breathe, it is not in a form that is usable to plants, so plants need to get their necessary nitrogen from an alternate source. Through the use of an Aquaponics system, plants can get nitrogen in the form that's suitable to them. This form of nitrogen is called Nitrate and it is made by bacteria that process Ammonia in order to grow. These bacteria are known as beneficial bacteria because they help achieve a positive outcome. Penicillin falls in this category. The more beneficial bacteria there is, the better it will be for your ecosystem because the fish release ammonia constantly through their waste and through their gills.

The bacteria eat the fish waste and process it, turning ammonia into nitrates for the plants to get fertilized.

When you first start your Aquaponics system, there are specific stages you take in which plants and fish are introduced. Before both, you will simply have water that will not only be used to test and make sure the system flows properly, but also to test for temperatures, oxygen, pH, and other balances. One of these tests which you will run periodically is to test for ammonia, nitrites, and nitrates. Obviously, we can't see bacteria because they are microscopic, so this test is very important. You might be thinking at this point:

- How can we be testing for something that comes out of fish when there are no fish?
- How can we introduce plants before fish, when fish feed the plants?

Both are good questions. Water in the tank right now will show no ammonia, no nitrites, and no nitrates, which as the question above pointed out, is a problem for the plants. It is not only a problem for the plants but also for the good bacteria we want to grow in our tank. If there is no ammonia, there will be no bacteria. As I said, this is a circle of life and we play Mother Nature so we must intervene and add ammonia so that there is a food source for bacteria. We essentially step in as substitutes for the fish until they can assume the role on a regular basis. We must monitor the process regularly and once we get to a level that works for our plants, then we can introduce them to the system. In the meantime, as we add ammonia, bacteria appear and start to do their job of converting it to nitrate. Our measurements will gradually show a decline in ammonia and a rise in nitrites. This is the level between ammonia and nitrates. Bacteria are doing its thing, but we are not quite there yet. Next, measurements will show a decrease further in ammonia, a decrease in nitrate, and now an increase in nitrate. Soon our measurements will reflect the necessary nitrate levels to effectively fertilize our plants and this means that bacteria levels are growing. This is good news and should only take about two weeks to achieve. This bacterial process is known as cycling. You know that your garden is fully cycled when there is a continual process of transforming ammonia into nitrite into nitrate. The addition of fish should maintain a fully cycled system.

Let us go back to the question about fish being introduced after plants. You could technically add plants and fish simultaneously as long as the ammonia levels have officially dropped to zero. Ammonia is poisonous to fish and though they are the ones producing it, they cannot live in it. Fish in an aquarium would have a filter to remove waste products to keep levels safe but in Aquaponics, we need to rely on the bacteria and the plants to keep the water safe for the fish.

Ammonia kits will advise proper levels and amount to add to your tank to ignite bacteria production and eventually nitrate. As each level is achieved through the cycle, less ammonia should be added. Generally, liquid ammonia is used and administered with a dropper. Another way to increase ammonia levels is to drop a few dead fish in the water since decomposing organisms release ammonia.

The intermediary level of the cycle, nitrite, usually occurs in the second week of the process. Though it is not quite as lethal as ammonia, it is important to continue measuring these levels until you reach the third level, nitrate, where it is beneficial to plants and safe for fish. During this nitrite cycle, do not add fish because nitrites stop blood from oxygen absorption and can cause gastrointestinal, renal, and nervous system failures. Because oxygen absorption is prevented, fish can stop breathing regardless of the oxygen supply available in their water.

Plants and fish will both benefit from the nitrate level of the cycle. Once your plants are consuming the nitrates, and you are in full cycle, your measurements may reflect zero on all three levels of the cycle once again: ammonia, nitrite, and nitrate.

**Mineralization**
The process by which chemical compounds are broken down in organic matter for plants to utilize is known as mineralization. The media surfaces of your garden are highly conducive to this process since the water and waste from the tank flows through their

regularly, allowing for the transformation into minerals and nutrients to occur naturally.

**Other Additives**
Ammonia is added to achieve cycling but there are other things you could add to help your plants flourish. Adding chelated iron powder will help the plants convert light to energy and look vibrant and full. Another additive would be kelp or seaweed because they have a host of vitamins and minerals needed by plants.

# CHAPTER 6
## *How to Do It Yourself*

Though it can be time-consuming and a bit daunting at times, it is extremely rewarding to be able to say you did it yourself and yes, it works! Believe me, it will be so worth it, in the end, knowing that you did your part for the environment and have the ability to successfully sustain your family through the food cultivated in an Aquaponics garden that you created with your bare hands!

Okay, so let's get started creating the environment for your own Aquaponic ecosystem. The main components of this ecosystem structure are the fish tank or tanks, the grow bed(s), and plumbing. Having the correct pieces for the puzzle and putting them together properly is vital for the living elements of your garden to flourish.

As you have read in the previous chapters, there are several options to choose from for your set up and functionality. This chapter will cover all of those options and functions so that you have the details needed to create your Aquaponic ecosystem as you wish to. The first thing to consider is the fish tank. It is important to determine whether you want to start big or small. If you want a small system, then a regular aquarium of about 10 or 20 gallons would suffice. If you want to go for the gold and go big, you need something with the capacity to contain a few hundred gallons of water, at least. This is not determined by what you wish to do with the fish (whether you are eating them or not), but how large a production of vegetables, herbs, and/or fruits you wish to have. Remember that no matter the size, any piece used in this puzzle must meet the standards of food/drinking water safety. If you do happen to find an aquarium that meets your capacity and cost requirements, you will need to take added measures to protect its inhabitants. First, it is wise to have a tank cover and secondly, additional filtration and aeration must be used to assist the plants in keeping the fish happy and healthy. These added items will protect them from algae, reduced oxygen levels, and overexposure (to light sources and peering eyes).

Some people choose to avoid the added expenses of the aquarium set up and enjoy taking on do it yourself to the level of building everything from scratch, increasing the amount of work and time involved for sure, but also the level of creative freedom. This avenue will allow for more control over your piggy bank as well as how much recycling and reusing actually gets incorporated into this process. There are numerous items you can use to build your tank and grow beds such as plastic barrels, IBC's, stock tanks, bathtubs, fish pond containers, and more. The list is long but what you choose depends on needs, size, whether you are indoors or out, appearance, cost, ability to locate specific supplies and ability to transport those supplies. So many variables!

**Some Options:**
One popular money-saving option is to use plastic barrels, otherwise known as 55-gallon drums. Though there are several color options for these however blue is the ideal option for the Aquaponics gardener due to its ability to block sun exposure and because blue barrels are specifically made to carry food products which makes it safe to use for your system. These barrels can be used for both the fish tank and the garden grow beds so they will need to be cut accordingly which means you will need to break out the jigsaw. As an option, these items are easy to find and easy to transport due to size and weight. Though they are not pretty to look at, they can be used inside or out. Some people choose to decorate the exterior when using indoors.

Another option is the IBC (Intermediate Bulk Container).

- Holds 275 gallons or more
- Wrapped in a metal cage
- Much more difficult to transform to a fish tank, sump tank, or grow bed—heavy duty tools needed!
- 48 inches tall on average
- Takes up a lot of yard space
- Need a truck to transport
- IBC tote kits are available at Aquaponics store
- To make building easier, you can visit backyardaquaponics.com to learn how

Stock tanks are made from sturdy plastic and can be found at agriculture or hardware chain stores.

- Considerably less expensive than an aquarium of the equivalent size which would cost about ten times more
- Fit in an SUV or van versus needing a truck
- Only 25 inches tall, making it ideal for the multilevel capability of grow beds over tanks and ease of access
- Can be purchased in assorted sizes
- A 50-gallon stock tank is usually about 12 inches high, which is an ideal height requirement for your garden grow beds
- The rounded shape of the stock tank is ideal for water circulation removing the ability to have dead zones that would likely occur in a rectangular aquarium set up

Specialty tanks like pond shells are made specifically for fish to thrive and can have over 1000 gallons in capacity. Additionally, they can be specially made with viewing areas so that you can see your fish. This can be a great option however it is important to consider that retailers in the United States are scarce still when it comes to Aquaponic specific items and therefore prices and shipping can be high.

As I stated earlier, the options are many and after you read this book or physically build your first system, you may come up with your own ingenious, creative ideas on how to set up your Aquaponics garden. You will have the knowledge to do so with confidence.

I will discuss how to create your system using stock tanks and also show you how to do so with plastic barrels in two formats: with sump pump and without. One format is a vertical, more compact set up that doesn't require a stand, and saves space, and the other format is a side by side setup that takes up more area. Keep in mind, when setting any Aquaponics system indoors, you must add proper lighting and maintain proper temperatures. Weight also needs to be taken into consideration. For your outdoor setups, you may want to consider some type of coverage like a greenhouse for added protection from the elements and pests. Another note if you want to cultivate plants which need to grow high and/or wide, you need to provide additional support and structures. Considering a pergola may be a good idea and they are not difficult to build if you prefer not to purchase one.

**Here are some specifics on the various parts you would use:**

### Bulkhead Fittings & Standpipes

Bulkhead fittings are used in plumbing done specifically in liquid storage. They are made so that a connection can pass through a watertight wall. These items have three main components: The threaded male part that projects through the watertight wall, also known as a bulkhead; The threaded female part that screws onto the male part; and a gasket to form enough pressure to prevent leakage. A bulkhead fitting is purposely made to allow pipes to connect from to another for water passage. The standpipe is a pipe that is vertical and extends from a supply of water. This pipe is placed inside the bulkhead fitting. As the water rises in the grow bed, where your standpipe is placed and reaches the top of the standpipe, the water will flow over it and out of the grow bed.

### Uniseal

Uniseal is a rubber O shaped gasket that fits right into a hole and can be used as an alternative to the bulkhead fitting accomplishing the same task of passing piping through a watertight seal.

### PVC

PVC is the most commonly used piping for plumbing because it is inexpensive, easy to work with, and easy to find.

### Irrigation Poly Tubing

Irrigation Poly Tubing is a very durable tubing used in irrigation however most cases not used in plumbing and therefore not safe for drinking water. Finding an exception in this category could prove very difficult.

### Garden Hose

Garden hoses can be a great use for Aquaponics however you must be mindful of which hoses are non potable, like the green ones which are very toxic. If you purchase the hose in 5/8" diameter, it will coincide with most of the fittings you have in your system and it is flexible so allows you to run it easily from one place to another.

### Vinyl Tubing
Black vinyl tubing is another great option for plumbing, however it is important to note that it needs to be securely attached to something, due to its tendency to move around when water pressure flows through it.

### Corrugated Tubing
Corrugated tubing is the fancy looking black vinyl tubing that has coils in it to prevent kinking. This tubing is very common and easy to find.

### Air Pumps
Air pumps come in many capacities however your Aquaponics system will need a specific air volume so purchasing one should be based on this criterion as opposed to water volume. These pumps are vital components to your system as they add much-needed oxygen to the water in your tank while circulating the water, which is also very important for the fish. I suggest purchasing one that has numerous outlets for more air flow.

### Diffusers
Diffusers are made to divide the air that flows from the air pump producing smaller bubbles and a wider area of air coverage. Air stones and line diffusers are popular types of diffusers used in Aquaponics systems.

### Water Pumps
Generally speaking, submersible water pumps are used in home Aquaponics systems. When purchasing a water pump, you need o make sure that the pump has the ability to circulate the entire volume of water in your Aquaponics system, every hour on the hour. The more powerful the better and though pumps are made for aquariums, it is more likely that you will get the proper pump if you purchase from a store that specializes in hydroponics or aquaponics. One last note would be that you should always remove the mesh filter from the pump to allow adequate flow.

### SLO

A solids lifting overflow is a type of standpipe that will remove the debris from the bottom of the fish tank while maintaining consistent water levels.

### Timers
This a device to turn things on and off and can be set for automatic time frames and apply to flood and drain, lighting, and more. Specialty stores will carry ones that can be programmed to repeat cycles.

### Indexing Valve
Used in conjunction with a timer that has repeat cycles, the indexing valve will move the flow of water from one inlet to many outlets and is commonly used when there are multiple grow beds. These valves based on settings will allow flow to one bed at a time and as one is done, it will close that outlet and open another.

### Auto Siphon
An auto siphon is made to automatically drain a container when the fluid level rises above the rim of the siphon and requires no electricity. The most popular siphons used are loop configuration and bell configuration. When using a loop siphon configuration, tubing is looped from the bottom of the media bed to the point at which you want the flood and drain to occur. When using the bell siphon configuration, the bell is placed over the standpipe itself and drains once the water reaches the top. Basically, a siphon occurs when the water overflows the standpipe and drains until air enters the bottom of the bell breaking the cycle of the siphon. The Affnan bell siphon has a funnel shape at the top to increase the amount of water flowing through the siphon. Coanda drains are also used in the siphon process since it connects the lower section with the drain section using a 45-degree connector causing the water flow to remain high and reduce obstruction.

Here are some options for system design:

### Aquaponics Design #1: 100-Gallon Stock Tank System
Supplies Needed:
- (2) 10-foot kiln dried 2x6 planks
- (2) 50-gallon stock tanks
- (1) 100-gallon stock tank

- (1) 1 x 3 board
- (1) 2 x 3 board
- (12) 8 x 8 x 16 concrete blocks
- (2) bulkhead fittings
- (2) Coanda drains with 2-inch lengths of PVC
- (2) Affnan-style standpipes
- (2) bell assemblies (2" PVC pipe and 2" PVC cap)
- (2) media guards
- (1) 25-foot 5/8" hose that is drinking water safe
- (2) female hose fittings
- (1) 400 gph (gallon per hour) water pump
- (1) plastic hose splitter
- (1) roll synthetic twine
- (1) air stone
- (1) ¼" vinyl air tubing
- (1) air check valve
- (1) small air pump
- 13 cubic feet of rocks from quarry

Tools Needed:
- Permanent Marker
- 1" spade drill bit, ¼" bit, and drill
- Miter saw
- Scissors

Start by preparing the frame. Place the two 2x6 planks on the ground about 4" apart. Place one of the 50-gallon grows beds on the planks, bottom side down. Mark, where the bottom of the grow bed, hits the planks to determine where to cut. Move the grow bed over about 4 feet and mark the planks again. Cut the planks with the miter saw and set aside. Trim the 2x6 scraps pieces so that they are 16 inches in length. Trim the 1x3 board and the 2x3 board into as many 16 inch pieces as you can. Next, position the fish tank and grow bed support system. Place the 100-gallon tank in the center of your space where it will be permanently positioned. Create two stacks of three concrete block stacks. Shim the planks with the 16 inch long boards you have cut. Next cut the holes in the grow beds to insert fittings. You will do this by turning the 50-gallon stock tanks upside down. Make a hole for the standpipe in the middle near one end using the 1" spade bit in the drill. The hole should be drilled in the bottom of each 50-gallon stock tank.

Assemble the bulkheads, Coanda drains, and standpipes in the beds. Assemble the bulkhead fittings in the hole through the bin. Put the male conduit connector through the whole first then slide the O-ring over the male pipe threads and then screw on the female conduit fitting. Stick the Coanda drain into the bottom of the bulkhead fittings. Stick the Affnan-style standpipe into the top of the bulkhead fitting. A 5 1/2" PVC pipe is a good length for connecting the fittings to the bulkhead. Position the 50-gallon stock tanks on the planks so the water will drain into the fish tank. These will be your grow beds. Place the PVC bell assemblies over the standpipes and slide the media guards over the bell portion of the standpipe drain.

Assemble the water pump and tubing. Cut the hose about 2 feet away from the male fitting. Cut two more lengths of hose about 7 feet long. Attach the cut end of the short hose to the pump. If the pump has a mesh or foam filter pad inside, remove it. Attach the hose splitter to the male end of the hose connected to the pump. Connect the female hose fittings to each of the 7-foot hose sections. Connect the 7-foot hose sections to the hose splitter. Make sure the splitter levers are turned in a direction that allows water to flow out.

Connect the hose to the fish tank and grow beds. Use the twine to connect the splitter to the fish tank. Use the twine to fasten the hoses so they will add water to the far end of each grows bed. You want the water coming in at the opposite side of the grow beds from where it will drain out. The length of twine should be sufficient enough to tie the hose along the side of the grow bed.

Assemble the air pump, tubing, and air stone by pushing the air stone onto the ¼" tubing. Clip a small portion of the tubing to use later on. Push the other end of the short length of tubing onto the opposite end of the check valve. Next, push the free portion of short tubing onto the air pump and place the air stone into the fish tank.

It's time to add media and water and turn the system on to conduct testing. First, rinse the stones one bucket at a time and add the rinsed stones to the grow beds. Add water to the system and turn the pumps on, adjusting the levers on the hose splitters to reduce the flow rate if necessary. If the flow rate is too high, your siphon cycle won't break. Once you see that everything is working properly and water tests are reading properly, you can move forward with plants and fish. This system should hold up to 15 fish at around a pound each when matured.

**Aquaponics Design #2: Plastic Barrel**
Supplies Needed:
- (1) 55-gallon BLUE barrel
- (1) 200 gph water pump
- Grow Medium
- (1) T fitting
- ½" PVC piping
- (2) #18 O-rings for grow bed connections
- (2) #14 O-rings for intake connections
- (1) ¾" PVC pipe 6" long for bell siphon
- (2) ¾" 90-degree elbow for the drain pipe
- (2) ¾" PVC pipe 4" long
- (1) ¾" male adapter threaded to slip for grow bed connections
- (1) ¾" female adapter threaded to slip for grow bed connections
- (1) ½" male adapter threaded to slip for intake connections
- (1) ½" female adapter threaded to slip for intake connections
- (1) ¾" to 1 ½" Bell Adapter
- (1) 2" PVC pipe 10" long for bell dome
- (1) 2" PVC pipe cap for bell dome
- (1) 3" PVC pipe 12" long for gravel guard

Tools Needed:
- Anything you prefer to use to cut holes into plastic PVC and slice barrels, like a Drill, Dremel or jigsaw
- 1/8" Drill bit
- 100% silicone and caulk gun

- Sandpaper (or rotary filing tool like a Bur)
- Sharpie

The barrel needs to be cut into two parts. Lay the barrel on its side and measure 12 inches from the top to cut around the barrel and remove one-third of it for the grow beds. The bottom two-thirds remaining will be used for the fish tank. After cutting, you want to smooth the edges with either sandpaper or a Bur, if you have one. Once you have smoothed the cut areas, wash out the barrels for added safety measures.

On the grow bed portion of your set up, you will need to make holes for the bell siphon and intake hose. Flip the bottom of the grow bed portion upside down and make your diameter measurements to match the actual parts being used. Once you have determined the size that the holes need to be to ensure a snug fit around pipes and hoses, use the Dremel to drill out your desired holes. Make sure you set the two holes on opposite sides of the grow bed container. Once holes are made, smooth out the cut surface.

Next, you will need to measure two holes to be cut in the fish tank portion of the barrel. One hole will be for fish viewing and access and the other hole will be for the power cord of the water pump. Some barrels have markings on them that tell you where the 30-gallon mark would be. If the barrel that you have purchased does not have this marking, simply measure about 16 ¾" from the bottom of the fish tank. This will be where you mark your water line. The next step will be to determine what shape you want for your viewing window. Some people have used fish or whale shapes, but an oval or circle will work just fine. Use a pre-made template or plastic plate to ensure that you outline the cutting line with a sharpie exactly the size and shape you wish. Remember to make sure that you set this area above the water level and leave a bit of space from the top as well (maybe two inches for both). Once you have done this, use your jigsaw, Dremel or whatever tool works for you, and cut out the viewing area. The next hole will be smaller since it is simply for cord passage, maybe the size of a plastic soup bowl. This hole will also need to be placed above the water zone. This should be followed by smoothing out the rough areas of your cut outs.

In order to attach the grow bed portion to the fish tank portion, you will need to make eight small holes that are equally spaced out around the very top of the fish tank. This will be attached to the grow bed with zip ties so that gives you an idea of diameter of the holes, but also means that you must place eight small holes on the lip at the bottom of the grow bed that line up exactly to the fish tank holes. Once you have done this, run the zip ties through each hole and tighten the grow bed to the fish tank. Cut the excess zip tie section off after you have secured everything together.

Now that the frame is built, you need to install the plumbing mechanisms. In order to do so, you will start by building your bell siphon. Take the male adapter and slip a #18 o-ring over the threads. Insert the adapter through the access hole that you have made in your grow bed. Slip another #18 o-ring over the top of the male threads. Screw the female and male adapters together ensuring that there is a tight connection. Slip a four to a six-inch piece of ¾" PVC pipe into the female adapter. The length will be determined by the water height so start at six and cut down to four if necessary. Slip the ¾" to 1 ½" bell adapter on top of the ¾" PVC pipe. To create an effective drain flow, it is important that the opening of the Bell is double the size of the pipe. Slide the PVC bell dome, 10" (can be adjusted to a shorter length if need be), over the drain pipe and the PVC gravel guard over this. For the side of the grow bed facing the fish, slide a piece of ¾" pipe into the bottom of the male adapter. Slide a ¾" PVC pipe and 90-degree elbow into the bottom of this pipe and then repeat with another ¾" PVC pipe and another 90-degree elbow.

The next step is to build the intake mechanism. Just as you did for the bell siphon, you will make a watertight seal in the hole you created using the male and female adapters, ½" this time, and the #14 O-rings. Place the water pump in the bottom of the fish tank (run the electrical cord out of the rear hole you created) and connect it to the bottom of the ½" adapter with a piece of ½" PVC pipe. The pump line will run about ten inches into the top of the intake adapter in the grow bed. Attach this to a T fitting and cap any openings. It is important to drill a tiny hole into the horizontal section of the pipe to let some water out. Check the flow rate when testing and add another tiny hole or two, if necessary.

Now that your plumbing is in place, you will run the system with the water in the tank and check the intake flow rate, drain rate, and potential leaks. If the bungee holes have leaks, seal the leaks with the silicon. Once you are satisfied that your system is working correctly, you can add your medium to the grow bed and test for blockages.

Once all of this is complete, you may then move on to cycling the system for the proper introduction of your plants and fish.

**Aquaponics Garden #3 Plastic Barrel with Stand, Sump, and Lighting**
Supplies needed:
- 10 feet of one inch PVC
- 3 feet of three inch PVC cut into two eighteen inch lengths
- (4) slip elbows for one inch PVC
- (1) T fitting for one inch PVC
- (2) end caps for one inch PVC
- (2) eight foot 2x6 pressure treated wood that should be cut into (6) thirty-inch lengths
- (2) eight foot 2x8 pressure treated wood that should be cut into (6) thirty-inch lengths
- (4) ten foot 2x4 pressure treated wood that should be cut into (4) 64-inch lengths and (4) 33-inch lengths
- (2) ten foot 2x4 pressure treated wood that should be cut into (4) 54 ½" inch lengths
- (2) eight foot 1x2 pressure treated wood that should be cut into (4) 48-inch lengths
- (4) sixty-inch lengths of metal chain
- (2) twelve-inch lengths of metal chain
- (4) S-hooks
- 300 gph water pump
- 20 feet of ½" flexible non-toxic tubing (drinking water safe)
- Metal Clamps
- Metal C-clamp
- (2) forty-eight-inch fluorescent shop lights with plugs

- (2) cool forty-eight-inch bulbs
- (2) warm forty-eight-inch bulbs
- (8) cinder blocks
- Twine
- Box of 2" deck screws
- Power Strip
- Timer
- Aquarium aerator with four nozzles
- (4) air stones
- 20 feet of airline tubing
- (2) ¾" to ½" tubing barb bulkhead fittings
- (1) Uniseal for 1" PVC
- Aquarium heater for 100-gallon tank
- (4) BLUE plastic barrels
- A ¼ cubic yard of Kenlite (or another medium)

Tools Needed:
- Power Drill
- Drill bit ¼"
- Drill hole saw bit 1.75" and 1.375"
- Jig Saw

The first step in the building process is to prepare the blue barrels. Each barrel has a different purpose and therefore needs to be prepared differently. The first barrel will be prepared for use as a fish tank. To start, lay the barrel on its side and cut a rectangular hole in the center measuring 13" x 23". Next, you will need to drill a hole on the circular side of the barrel using a 1.75" hole saw. The hole should be located approximately 4" from the lip of the barrel and lined up with the hole that you cut on the side. Make sure any rough edges are smoothed. Make sure to wash the barrels. Place the 1" Uniseal through the hole. Next, you will need to cut the rectangular window in the side of the barrel for the sump tank as well. It is important that both the fish tank barrel and the sump tank barrel have securely plugged bungholes, due to the fact that they will be containing water and you want to avoid leaks. The third barrel is going to be used for the grow beds so you just need to cut the barrel in half, lengthwise. Measure 1 inch from the lip of the barrel and drill a hole, with the 1.375 holes saw bit, on the bottom of each of these halves. Thread the barbed bulkhead fitting through the hole in each. Attach it so that the ½" barbed fitting is on the outside of the half tank and make sure that the bulkhead is flush on the inside. The last tank will be used as a water reserve for topping off evaporated water in your system. For this, simply remove the top. It will remain standing upright. The water will be aerated and transferred as needed over time.

The next thing you will need to prepare is the frame that will hold the tanks and grow beds. Two of each length of 2x4 boards need to be combined. Use the deck screws to secure two 2x4's together to achieve 4x4's in length of 33, 54.5, and 64 inches. Create a V shape by attaching the 30-inch 2x6 boards and 30-inch 2x8 boards using deck screws. The mouth of the V created should be about ten inches in width. You will need to build 6 altogether. Position three of the V's face down (one on each end and one in the center) onto the 54.5 inches long 4x4, about 12 inches apart, to create the grow bed stand. Next, lay out the two 30 inch pieces of lumber so that they are parallel to each other, about 30 inches apart. With the V facing down, position one on each end and attach them to the 54.5-inch boards using the deck screws. Drill the screws through the outer edge of the V into the board on both sides. This will be used as the fish tank stand. Cinder blocks need to be set up at the corners of an area measuring 36 x 56 inches. Place the second set of cinder blocks on top of these. Take the 64 inch 4x4's and place them the 56-inch length of the area on the cinder blocks. The grow bed stand will sit atop of the 64 inch 4x4 with Vs facing forward. This should be flush at the edge of the 64 inch 4x4 putting the grow bed stands towards the front portion of the 64 inch 4x4. The fish tank stand will be placed at the back end of the 64 inch 4x4 with the V's perpendicular to the grow beds, flush to the back edge of 64 inch 4x4. Position a 48-inch length of 1x2 to the corner of the grow bed stand, keeping the bottom of the board flush with the bottom of the 54.5 inch 4x4. The 2-inch width of the board should be along the 30-inch side of the grow bed stand. Use deck screws to attach the board in place. Do this to all four corners. Attach a single screw to the top of each of this 1x2's with a small portion of the screw sticking out for light fixtures to attach to later on.

Now that the frame has been built, you can place the grow beds and the fish tank on their respective stands with the V's as support structures. The sump tank will be placed on the floor in front of the grow bed stand and supported by the remaining V facing down.

Now, it's time to work on the plumbing. Cut a short section of 1 inch PVC pipe, approximately 3 inches in length. Push this section through the Uniseal in the fish tank so that only 1-inch sticks into the tank with the remainder sticking out. Add an L connector to the end of this piece so that the next PVC pipe will go straight down along the side of the tank. Cut another piece of PVC approximately 4 inches in length and attach it to the L connector, ending about midway down the height of the fish tank. Add another L connector to the end of this piece to change the direction to head towards the Grow Beds. Cut a 4-inch section of PVC to slip into the L connector and travel beyond the edge of the fish tank. Add another L connector to the end of this piece to change the direction to wrap around the midsection of the tank. This will make the next piece of PVC travel along the length of the fish tank. Cut a 16-inch length of PVC and fit it into the L connector. This piece should end roughly near the midpoint of the long dimension of the fish tank. Add a final L connector to the end of the PVC to change the direction to point away from the fish tank and towards the grow beds. Cut a final 4-inch section of PVC and slip it into the L. It should end over the Grow Beds, running between the two halves. Add a T connector to the end of the pipe to split the flow between the two grow beds. If necessary, add a short section of PVC to each side of the T so that water flows into the grow beds rather than into the space between the two beds.

Using a ¼" drill bit, drill a hole into the end wall of each grow bed half barrel tank near the upper edge. This should be on the same side near the bulkhead fitting sticking out of the bottom. Attach a 24-inch section of ½" black vinyl tubing onto the barbed end of the bulkhead fitting in the grow bed half barrel tank. If needed, you can use a metal clamp, to secure this tubing on so that it doesn't leak from the barbed fitting. Thread a 12-inch section of twine through the ¼" hole at the top of the half tank. Twist the vinyl tube into a loop so that the other end of the tube end hangs above the sump tank below. Hold it in place by looping the string through the highest point of the tube and tying it in a knot. The highest part of the tube should be approximately 2 inches from the top lip of the half tank and this will be the high water mark of the grow beds. Do the same process to the other half tank. Using a metal clamp, attach the end of the remaining black vinyl tubing to the outflow of the water pump. Place the pump in the bottom of the Sump tank. Snake the tubing along the outside of the sump tank and grow beds and up the side of the fish tank so that it ends up at the opening of the fish tank. This will return the water from the sump tank back to the fish tank. You can attach the tubing to the fish tank using a metal C clamp.

Using one of the 18-inch lengths of 3-inch diameter PVC, center it on the hole in the grow bed that leads to the bulkhead fitting and the loop siphon. Holding this pipe in place, fill the bed with either of the suggested mediums discussed in this book until it is 1 inch below the rim of the half tank. Do the same for the second grow bed? Install the heater so that it rests in the fish tank. This can be dangled into the fish tank through the opening on the top. Run two lengths of airline tubing with air stones from the air pump to the fish tank. This will provide the necessary oxygen to your fish. Run two more lengths of airline tubing with air stones from the air pump to the extra water tank that will be used for topping off. This aeration will help dissipate the chlorine from the tap water.

From this point, you begin testing systemic functions, and then cycling. Once everything is all set, you may add your fish and plants. Once plants are added, make sure to turn on the lights and if you wish, set them to a timer to ensure proper amounts of day and night. The lights will be attached to the posts you set up on the four corners of your frame.

## An Alternate Option to Media Bed Systems:
Aside from the various ways to create a media bed system, there are numerous ways to get creative with the Nutrient Film Technique also. This may be an option you are considering and many utilize PVC piping to create rows or even levels of grow beds in varying sizes. Depending on your set up, plumbing for these systems would differ greatly and would need to be adapted accordingly. In my opinion, these systems tend to be better suited for herbs and smaller vegetation. If used for vegetation that will become sizable, the plants will need to be transplanted at a certain

point in their growth process. I prefer to maintain a system in which the plants can grow through their entire cycle.

**Maintenance**
Now that you have the basics down and your Aquaponics garden seems to be running smoothly, you will want to keep it that way so there are general maintenance steps to perform daily, weekly, monthly and seasonally. This chapter will cover these steps as well as advise on how to perform certain maintenance tests. I highly recommend keeping an agenda book where you maintain logs, to do list, supply lists, vendor contacts, and calendar. This will make life so much easier. Staying organized will remove stress factors like remembering what to do and when, allowing you to enjoy the benefits of a healthy, productive garden with an abundance of healthy fish.

**Daily**
- Feed fish
- Check water
    - Temperature
    - Level
- Check plants
    - Growth
    - Pests

These are important to check regularly because if the temperatures are off, it can greatly affect your fish including feeding habits. If food is put in the tank and fish don't eat it, it will accumulate and can raise the ammonia levels that are toxic to fish. A proper environment will have healthy fish eating all food within a five-minute time span. Checking the water levels is also important due to the potential evaporation. Distilled water is pH neutral, so it is the best option to top off the tank. Since everything in an Aquaponics system affects the other, you want to check on your plants too. Make sure there aren't any pests nibbling on your plants and check to see if any plants are ready to be harvested.

**Weekly**
- Check pH, oxygen, ammonia, nitrite, and nitrate levels.
- Check plumbing for any clogs and make sure everything is running smoothly.

- Prune plants.

**Monthly**
- Purchase supplies
- Purchase seeds
- Check pump and make sure everything is clear and running as it should be.

**Seasonal/ Annual**
- Change plants to correspond with the correct season
- Renew any licenses you may need (most expire annually, and each state has its own requirements)
- Work on budget planning for following season/ year
- Determine if you are going to expand or if you need to make more fish purchases
- Make any repairs to Aquaponics area such as greenhouse
- Harvest fish to eat or freeze for a later date

**Pest Control**

Your garden can be your answer to fresh healthy eating, "farm to table". You grow your garden to feed your family, not to feed pests. Even if your garden is ornamental, that beauty and all that work should not be wasted on pests. Here are some solutions:

- Fight fire with fire. Some bugs are indeed good bugs for your garden.
    - Ladybugs eat a long list of the most common garden pests
    - Lacewings are also known to eat most common garden pests
    - Praying Mantises love to eat and are great bug hunters.
- There are some plants that are insect repellants
    - Marigolds: bugs hate the smell and taste (especially mosquitoes and aphids)
    - Garlic and chives keep slugs away
    - Peppermint is a great ant repellant
    - Lavender deters flying and crawling insects and it smells great.

- Of course, you can always go with the traditional bug zappers, sticky strips, and/or a safe bacteria known as BT or Bacillus thuringiensis
- 

## Maintenance Tests

It is extremely important to take care of the ecosystem that you have created. If you care for your system, the system will return the favor to you in abundance. One of the best purchases you can make and ironically one of the less expensive items will be a freshwater master test kit. This kit will have everything included that is necessary to conduct enough tests, throughout the year, for pH, ammonia, nitrites, and nitrates and will take only five minutes of your time. Each kit will advise the proper way to conduct the test and the results desired. This section covers all of the tests that you will need to conduct and how to conduct them.

## pH

Changes can happen very quickly in the system and therefore testing the pH balance is important each month. If the pH test demonstrates that the water is not neutral, meaning it is higher in either acid or alkaline, you will need to create balance again. In order to reduce the alkalinity levels because they are registering over 7.0 (neutral), you would need to add some acid to the water until the levels go down to neutral readings. The suggested acid additive would be hydrochloric acid which can be easily purchased at any home and garden improvement store. Instead of adding the HCL directly to the water in the fish tank, it is advised that you add it to grow beds so that they can do their necessary biofiltration process which will be much safer for your fish. It is also important to remember not to use products specifically made for Aquariums because of their tendency to have high levels of sodium which could be highly detrimental to your plants. The opposite can also occur and you may find that you need to increase your pH levels (lower than 7.0 neutral reading) because there is too much acid present in the fish tank water. Bicarbonate or Hydroxide compounds of potassium and calcium will aid in increasing your bases and reducing the acid readings. While they neutralize your levels, they work to improve the health of your plants because they are necessary nutrients for your garden. Again, the compound you choose should be administered through the grow beds and not directly into the fish tank water.

**Dissolved Oxygen**
As discussed earlier, there are definite signs that there is an issue with the oxygen levels in your fish tank water. Your fish may not speak with words, but they can tell you volumes if you pay attention to them and one clear sign that there is an oxygen deficiency is when the fish seem to be gasping for air and spending most of their time at the top of the water. Either way, if the fish are acting funky, something is wrong in the water so you will need to run tests. If it is the oxygen versus one of the other levels being out of whack, simply run an air pump to increase air flow. Additionally, your plant to fish ratios may need to be adjusted by increasing your grow beds. A popular and efficient kit for testing the dissolved oxygen levels is made by Salifert.

You will also need to monitor your temperature, humidity, light and the water levels, as these can impact the readings of other things you are testing for.

**Ammonia, Nitrite, and Nitrate**
As discussed earlier, vital to the health of your plants and fish, maintaining a proper Nitrogen Cycle is so important. The same kit that advised to purchase for pH testing, will give you enough tests to conduct throughout the course of a year for each of these categories as well. If you find that the levels are not at zero which would be evident in a full cycle, then you will need to add minimal amounts of ammonia until the cycle completes and your readings reflect zero ammonia, zero nitrites, and either have nitrate or are in full cycle again reading nitrate at zero.

# CONCLUSION

Thank you for making it through to the end of Aquaponics: Beginner's Guide To Building Your Own Aquaponic Garden System That Will Grow Organic Vegetables, Fruits, Herbs and Raising Fish With Your Own Aquaponics Home Gardening System. Let's hope it was informative and able to provide you with all of the tools you need to achieve your goals, whatever they may be.

The next step is to either purchase your Aquaponics kit or if you choose to go down the DO IT YOURSELF path, purchase a blueprint or design your own structure. Whatever path you choose, in order to embark on your first Aquaponics journey, you are now equipped with the basics to be successful growing your own Aquaponics garden and reaping the rewards of a bountiful harvest and healthy fresh fish to eat.

As you now know, Aquaponics is not simply about the food you eat but it is also about your contribution to the environment, how much money you can save, and how much pleasure and satisfaction Aquaponics gardening gives you when you accomplish your first harvest. I am hoping this book will continue to guide you along your journey as it can be referenced every step of the way. Always be mindful of the ecosystem you have created and all of the living organisms that inhabit it. Remember that you are stepping in as Mother Nature and the plants, fish, and bacteria are your responsibility to nurture and protect. As long as you do, they will be good to you in return and continue to feed you for years to come!

Finally, if you found this book useful in any way, a review on Amazon is always appreciated!

# DESCRIPTION

In a world where we must be concerned with so many potentially negative occurrences environmentally, politically, or otherwise, and are surrounded by many potentially harmful things or vices that may or may not be out of our control, it is reassuring to know that there is one way that we can take back some degree of power over the outcome. It may seem insignificant in the overall scheme of things at first, but making the choice to read this book Aquaponics: Beginner's Guide To Building Your Own Aquaponic Garden System That Will Grow Organic Vegetables, Fruits, Herbs and Raising Fish With Your Own Aquaponics Home Gardening System and learn what you can about Aquaponics, will create the stepping stones you need to start the change you desire in your life and in your family's life.

Every little bit that we do can count and it can impact not only ourselves but the world around us in both a positive or negative way. The choice you make today can be a very powerful one. This book does not just offer a wealth of knowledge but invites you to begin a wonderful journey to a new lifestyle. This new lifestyle will give you the ability to control the freshness of the foods you eat and the choice of which foods you have readily available to prepare for your meals, without leaving your home. Choosing this path will give you the peace of mind in knowing that what you are preparing has not been contaminated and offers you and your family a healthy option. This journey will also pave the way for you to take control of your physical and mental health due to your dietary choices.

Aquaponics is a great way to produce your own fish and plants not just simply for the benefit of a meal or saving the expense you would have if bought at a grocery store, but it is also an excellent way for you to wage battle against major illnesses.
The benefits of choosing Aquaponics are numerous but most are not aware of how it helps on a global level. There are many companies out there helping to improve the sustainability of the world as a whole, especially in areas where the soil is not conducive to farming and there is a lack of water and food but what many

people may not realize is that by doing Aquaponics at home, you are also helping the environment and can even help to improve the economy if you choose to expand this process into a business. Start your journey now by buying this book and you will reap the benefits easily, shortly thereafter!

**In this book, you will find**

- All the answers to your questions about what exactly Aquaponics is, how does it work and how does it differ from Hydroponics and Aquaculture. Is it really better?
- Everything you need to know to get started, whether you start with a kit or do it yourself
- This guide will explain in detail how to create the most ideal Aquaponics environment and the differences in using assorted types of grow beds, filtration, containment systems, plumbing, water, light, temperatures, etc.
- You will learn what types of fish and plants work best and gain a better understanding of their requirements and differences amongst the varying seasons. In addition to this, you will gain a good understanding of how to maintain your system so that you have a thriving ecosystem that is productive in providing sustenance for you and your family
- And much more!

www.ingramcontent.com/pod-product-compliance
Lightning Source LLC
Chambersburg PA
CBHW071505070526
44578CB00001B/445